FIRST 50
KIDS' SON
YOU SHOULD PLAY ON UKULELE

Front cover ukulele photo courtesy of Flight Instruments

ISBN 978-1-70515-120-4

HAL•LEONARD®

Visit Hal Leonard Online at
www.halleonard.com

Contact Us:
Hal Leonard
7777 West Bluemound Road
Milwaukee, WI 53213
Email: info@halleonard.com

In Europe, contact:
Hal Leonard Europe Limited
42 Wigmore Street
Marylebone, London, W1U 2RN
Email: info@halleonardeurope.com

In Australia, contact:
Hal Leonard Australia Pty. Ltd.
4 Lentara Court
Cheltenham, Victoria, 3192 Australia
Email: info@halleonard.com.au

CONTENTS

Animal Crackers in My Soup

from CURLY TOP
Lyrics by Ted Koehler and Irving Caesar
Music by Ray Henderson

Bridge

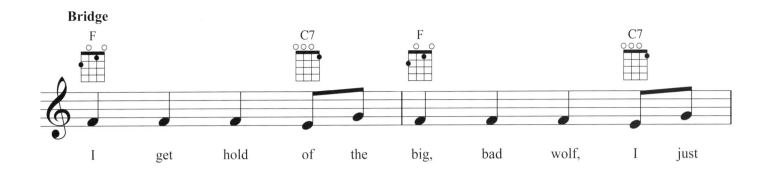

I get hold of the big, bad wolf, I just

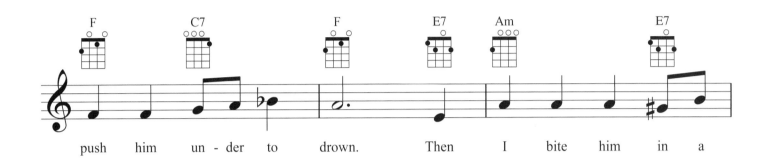

push him un - der to drown. Then I bite him in a

D.C. al Coda

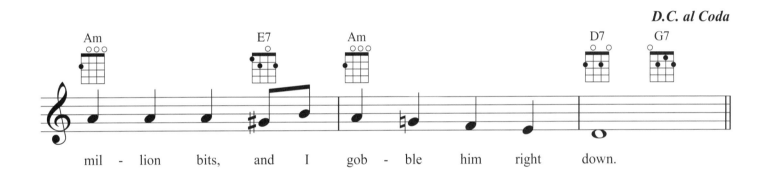

mil - lion bits, and I gob - ble him right down.

Coda

stuff my tum - my like a "goop," with

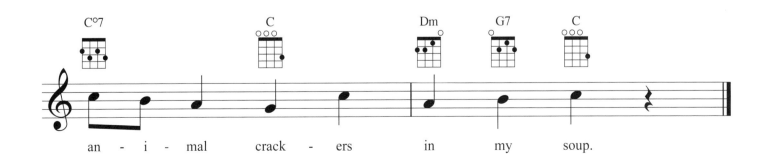

an - i - mal crack - ers in my soup.

Any Dream Will Do

from JOSEPH AND THE AMAZING TECHNICOLOR® DREAMCOAT

Music by Andrew Lloyd Webber
Lyrics by Tim Rice

Baby Shark

Traditional Nursery Rhyme
Arranged by Pinkfong and KidzCastle

First note

Verse

With a bounce

1. Ba - by   shark, do do do do ___ do do. Ba - by   shark, do do do do ___ do do. Ba - by
3., 5. *See additional lyrics*

shark, do   do   do do ___ do do. Ba - by   shark.   2. Mom - my
                                                               4., 6. *(See additional lyrics)*

Verse

shark, do do do do ___ do do. Mom - my   shark, do do do do ___ do do. Mom - my

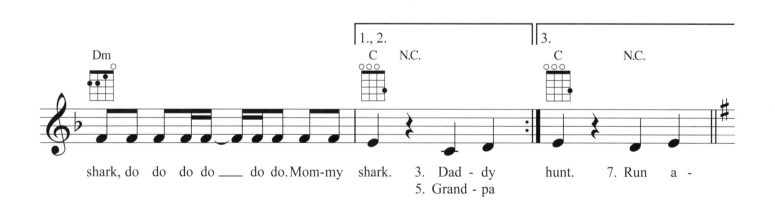

1., 2.   3.

shark, do do do do ___ do do. Mom-my shark.   3. Dad - dy   hunt.   7. Run a -
                                                  5. Grand - pa

Verse

way, do do do do ___ do do. Run a - way, do do do do ___ do do. Run a -
last, do do do do ___ do do. Safe at last, do do do do ___ do do. Safe at

1.

way, do do do do ___ do do. Run a - way.   8. Safe at
last, do do do do ___ do do. Safe at

2.   **Verse**

last. 9. It's the end, do do do do ___ do do. It's the end, do do do do ___ do do. It's the

end, do do do do ___ do do. It's the end.

Additional Lyrics

3. Daddy shark, do do do do do do.
   Daddy shark, do do do do do do.
   Daddy shark, do do do do do do.
   Daddy shark.

5. Grandpa shark, do do do do do do.
   Grandpa shark, do do do do do do.
   Grandpa shark, do do do do do do.
   Grandpa shark.

4. Grandma shark, do do do do do do.
   Grandma shark, do do do do do do.
   Grandma shark, do do do do do do.
   Grandma shark.

6. Let's go hunt, do do do do do do.
   Let's go hunt, do do do do do do.
   Let's go hunt, do do do do do do.
   Let's go hunt.

Bananas in Pyjamas

Words and Music by Carey Blyton

First note

Moderately · Verse

1. Ba - nan - as in py - jam - as are com - ing down the
(2.) chi - nis in bi - ki - nis are com - ing down the

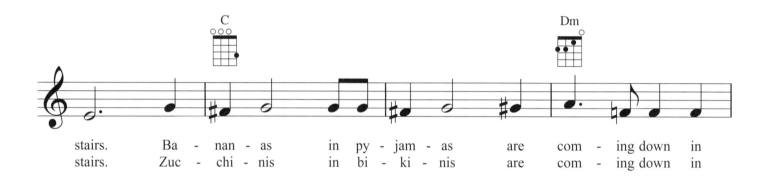

stairs. Ba - nan - as in py - jam - as are com - ing down in
stairs. Zuc - chi - nis in bi - ki - nis are com - ing down in

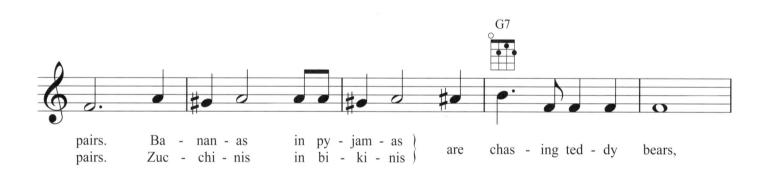

pairs. Ba - nan - as in py - jam - as } are chas - ing ted - dy bears,
pairs. Zuc - chi - nis in bi - ki - nis }

1.   2.

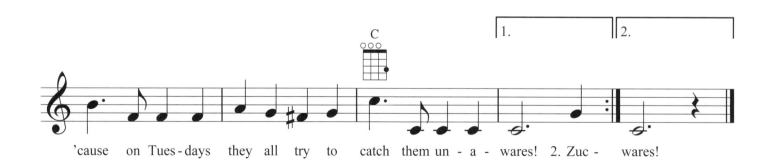

'cause on Tues - days they all try to catch them un - a - wares! 2. Zuc - wares!

Bingo

Traditional

Note: Each time a letter of BINGO
is deleted in the lyric, clap your hands
in place of singing the letter.

Bob the Builder

(Main Title)

Words and Music by Paul K. Joyce

First note

Intro
Moderately fast

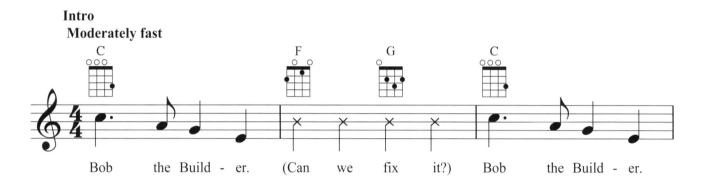

Bob   the   Build - er.   (Can   we   fix   it?)   Bob   the   Build - er.

Verse

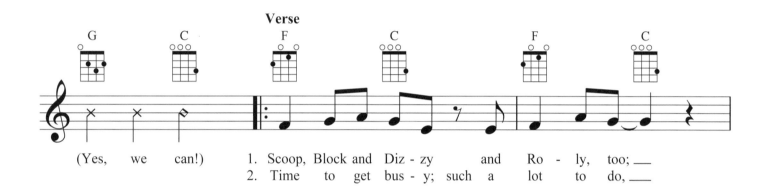

(Yes,   we   can!)

1. Scoop, Block and Diz - zy   and   Ro - ly,   too; ___
2. Time   to   get   bus - y;   such   a   lot   to   do, ___

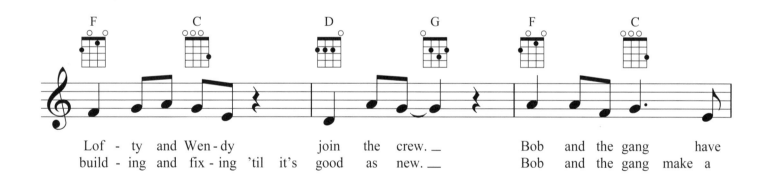

Lof - ty   and   Wen - dy   join   the   crew. _   Bob   and   the   gang   have
build - ing and fix - ing 'til   it's   good   as   new. _   Bob   and   the   gang   make a

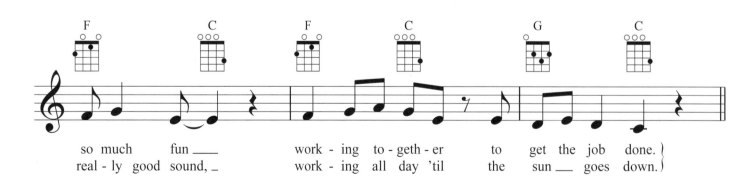

so   much   fun ___   work - ing to - geth - er   to   get   the   job   done.)
real - ly   good   sound, _   work - ing   all   day   'til   the   sun ___   goes   down.)

Chorus

Bob the Build - er. (Can we fix it?) Bob the Build - er.

(Yes, we can!) Bob the Build - er. (Can we fix it?)

Bob the Build - er. (Yes, we can!)

Outro-Chorus

Bob the Build - er. (Can we fix it?) Bob the Build - er.

(Oh.) Bob the Build - er. Can we fix it?

Bob the Build - er. (Yes, we can!)
(Instrumental)

"C" Is for Cookie

from the Television Series SESAME STREET
Words and Music by Joe Raposo

Verse
Moderately

1., 2., 4. C is for cook-ie, that's good e-nough for me! C is for cook-ie, that's
3. (Spoken:) A round cookie with one bite out of it looks like a C. A round doughnut with one

good e-nough for me! C is for cook-ie, that's good e-nough for me! Oh,
bite out of it looks like a C, *but it is not as good as a cookie.* *Oh, and the*

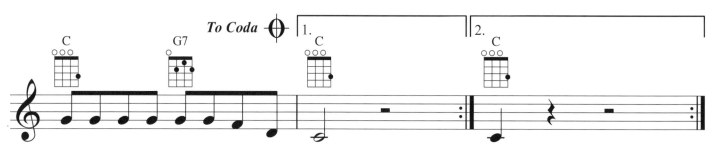

To Coda

1. 2.

cook-ie, cook-ie, cook-ie starts with C. C. (Spoken:) Hey, you know what?
moon sometimes looks like a C,

3. *D.C. al Coda* Coda

but you can't eat that. So C. Yeah! Cook-ie, cook-ie, cook-ie starts with

C. Oh boy! Cook-ie, cook-ie, cook-ie starts with C.

Dites-Moi
(Tell Me Why)

from SOUTH PACIFIC

Lyrics by Oscar Hammerstein II
Music by Richard Rodgers

Castle on a Cloud

from LES MISÉRABLES

Music by Claude-Michel Schönberg
Lyrics by Alain Boublil, Jean-Marc Natel and Herbert Kretzmer

Music and French Lyrics Copyright © 1980 by Editions Musicales Alain Boublil
English Lyrics Copyright © 1986 by Alain Boublil Music Ltd. (ASCAP)
Mechanical and Publication Rights for the U.S.A. Administered by Alain Boublil Music Ltd. (ASCAP) c/o Spielman Koenigsberg & Parker, LLP,
Richard Koenigsberg, 1675 Broadway, 20th Floor, New York, NY 10019, Tel 212-453-2500, Fax 212-453-2550, ABML@skpny.com

2. Am | F | C
cloud. There is a la - dy all in white, ___

F | C | B♭ | F
holds me and sings a lull - a - by. She's nice to see and she's soft to touch. She

E | Am | E F Dm E
rall. *a tempo*
says, "Co - sette, I love you ver - y much." I know a place where no one's

Am | G
lost. I know a place where no one

C | Dm | C | E
cries. Cry - ing at all is not al -

F | Dm | E | Am
rall.
lowed, not in my cas - tle on a cloud.

Do-Re-Mi

from THE SOUND OF MUSIC
Lyrics by Oscar Hammerstein II
Music by Richard Rodgers

Don't Give Up

from the Television Series SESAME STREET
Words by Joseph Mazzarino
Music by Bill Sherman

Try and try ___ and you'll come out on top. ___ Don't give up. ___

Verse

3. You got your-self some rol-ler-skates. _ You

put them on ___ and you ___ feel great. _ You stand up, but

then you fall. ___ You don't think you ___ can skate ___ at all. ___ You

get back up, and then you trip. ___ You skip and tip and

slip and flip. ___ Well, try and try and try some more, ___ and

soon you're skat - ing 'cross ___ the floor. ___

Chorus

Don't give ___ up. Keep ___ on mov - ing. You're

gon - na get ___ there; just keep on groov - ing. Don't give

up. ___ Don't ___ pack it in. ___ Try and try, ___ and you ___

Outro

___ will win. ___ Don't give up. ___ No ___ no no no, don't give

up. ___ No ___ no no no, don't give up. ___

Dora the Explorer Theme Song

from DORA THE EXPLORER

Words and Music by Joshua Sitron, Sarah B. Durkee and Billy Straus

Eensy Weensy Spider

Traditional

Een - sy, ween - sy spi - der went up the wa - ter -

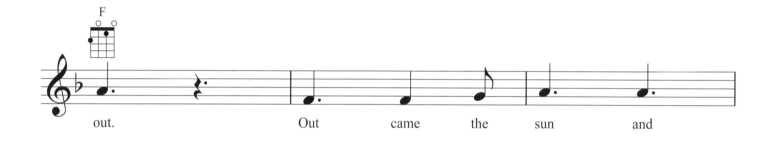

spout. Down came the rain and washed the spi - der

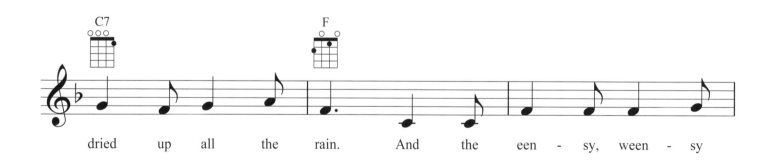

out. Out came the sun and

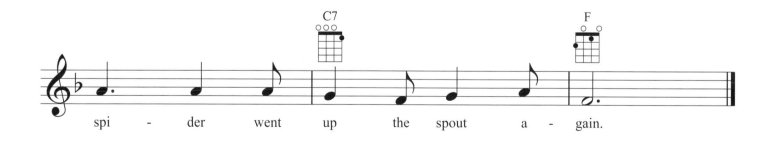

dried up all the rain. And the een - sy, ween - sy

spi - der went up the spout a - gain.

Hush, Little Baby

Carolina Folk Lullaby

Everything Is Awesome
(Awesome Remixx!!!)
from THE LEGO MOVIE

Words by Shawn Patterson
Music by Andrew Samberg, Jorma Taccone, Akiva Schaffer,
Joshua Bartholomew, Lisa Harriton and Shawn Patterson

First note

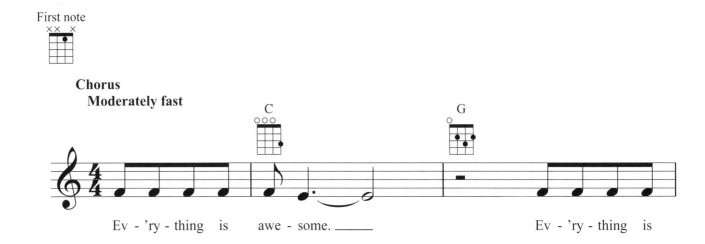

Ev - 'ry - thing is awe - some. _____ Ev - 'ry - thing is

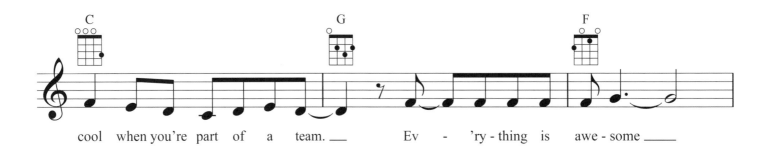

cool when you're part of a team. ___ Ev - 'ry - thing is awe - some ___

when we're liv - ing our ___ dream.

Bridge

Ev - 'ry - thing ___ is bet - ter when ___ we stick ___ to - geth - er. _

Side by side, __ you and I __ gon - na win __ for - ev -

- er. Let's par - ty for - ev - er. We're the same, _ I'm like you, _

__ you're like me. __ We're all work - ing in har - mo - ny. __

Outro-Chorus

__ Ev - 'ry - thing is awe - some. __ Ev - 'ry - thing is

cool when you're part of a team. __ Ev - 'ry - thing is awe - some __

when we're liv - ing our __ dream.

Happiness

from YOU'RE A GOOD MAN, CHARLIE BROWN
Words and Music by Clark Gesner

First note

Verse
Moderately

1. Hap - pi - ness is two kinds of ice cream,
2. Hap - pi - ness is five dif - f'rent cray - ons,

find - ing your skate key, tell - ing the time.
know - ing a se - cret, climb - ing a tree.

Hap - pi - ness is learn - ing to whis - tle, ty - ing your shoe for the
Hap - pi - ness is find - ing a nick - el, catch - ing a fire - fly, ___

ver - y first time. Hap - pi - ness is
set - ting him free. Hap - pi - ness is

Here We Go Looby Loo

Traditional Folk Song

First note

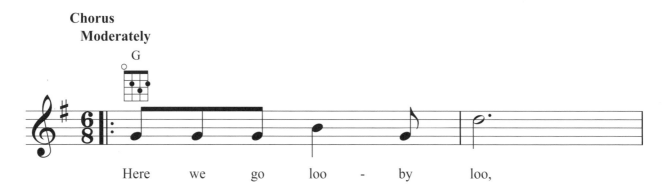

Here we go loo - by loo,

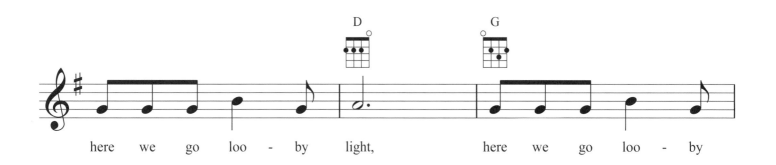

here we go loo - by light, here we go loo - by

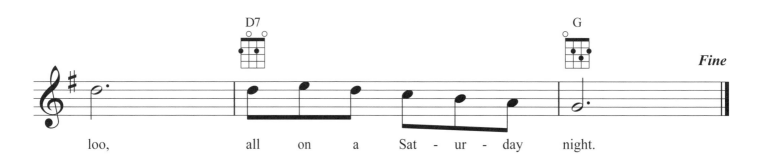

loo, all on a Sat - ur - day night. *Fine*

Verse

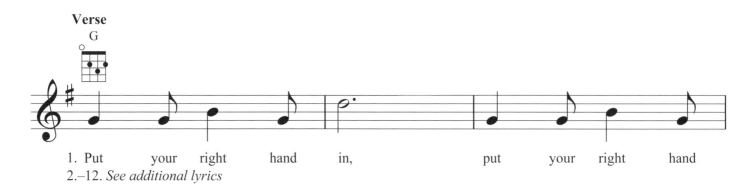

1. Put your right hand in, put your right hand
2.–12. *See additional lyrics*

out,   put   your   right   hand   in   a - gain   and

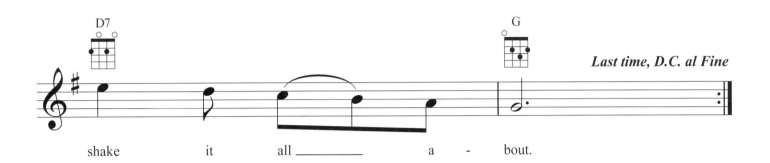

Last time, D.C. al Fine

shake   it   all _____ a - bout.

Additional Lyrics

2. Put your left hand in,
   Put your left hand out,
   Put your left hand in again
   And shake it all about.

3. Put your right arm in,
   Put your right arm out,
   Put your right arm in again
   And shake it all about.

4. Put your left arm in,
   Put your left arm out,
   Put your left arm in again
   And shake it all about.

5. Put your right foot in,
   Put your right foot out,
   Put your right foot in again
   And shake it all about.

6. Put your left foot in,
   Put your left foot out,
   Put your left foot in again
   And shake it all about.

7. Put your right leg in,
   Put your right leg out,
   Put your right leg in again
   And shake it all about.

8. Put your left leg in,
   Put your left leg out,
   Put your left leg in again
   And shake it all about.

9. Put your back in,
   Put your back out,
   Put your back in again
   And shake it all about.

10. Put your front in,
    Put your front out,
    Put your front in again
    And shake it all about.

11. Put your head in,
    Put your head out,
    Put your head in again
    And shake it all about.

12. Put your whole self in,
    Put your whole self out,
    Put your whole self in again
    And shake it all about.

Hot Dog!

from MICKEY MOUSE CLUB HOUSE
Words and Music by John Flansburgh and John Linnell

First note

Chorus

Moderately, in 2

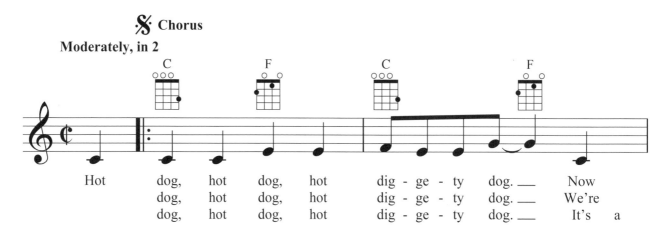

Hot dog, hot dog, hot dig - ge - ty dog. ___ Now
dog, hot dog, hot dig - ge - ty dog. ___ We're
dog, hot dog, hot dig - ge - ty dog. ___ It's a

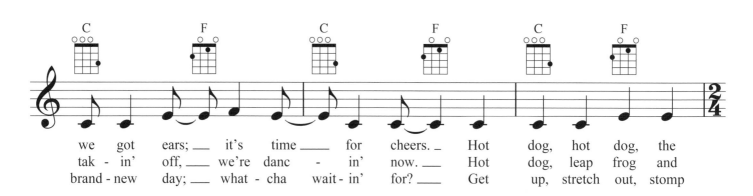

we got ears; ___ it's time ___ for cheers. ___ Hot dog, hot dog, the
tak - in' off, ___ we're danc - in' now. ___ Hot dog, leap frog and
brand - new day; ___ what - cha wait - in' for? ___ Get up, stretch out, stomp

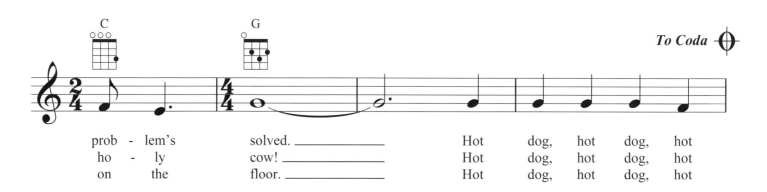

prob - lem's solved. _____ Hot dog, hot dog, hot
ho - ly cow! _____ Hot dog, hot dog, hot
on the floor. _____ Hot dog, hot dog, hot

Verse

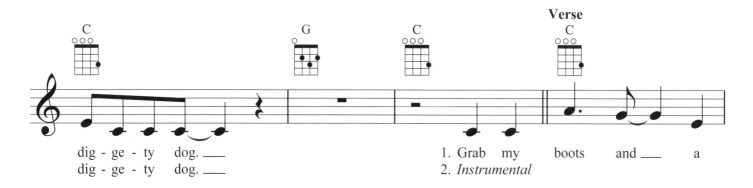

dig - ge - ty dog. ___ 1. Grab my boots and ___ a
dig - ge - ty dog. ___ 2. *Instrumental*

sand - wich; ___ let's start a ___ pa - rade. Get the

co - co - nut drum kit ___ for Dais - y ___ to

2nd time, D.S. al Coda

Coda

play.
Instrumental ends ⎫ Hot
dig - ge - ty dog. ___ Hot

Outro-Chorus

dog, hot dog, hot dig - ge - ty dog. ___ We're split - tin' the scene, we're

full of beans. ___ So long ___ for now ___ from Mick - ey

Mouse ___ and the Mick-ey Mouse Club - house!

How Far I'll Go

from MOANA
Music and Lyrics by Lin-Manuel Miranda

First note

Verse
Moderately

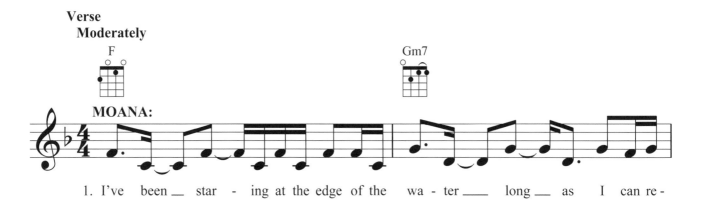

MOANA:

1. I've been __ star - ing at the edge of the wa - ter __ long __ as I can re -

mem - ber, __ nev - er real - ly know - ing why.

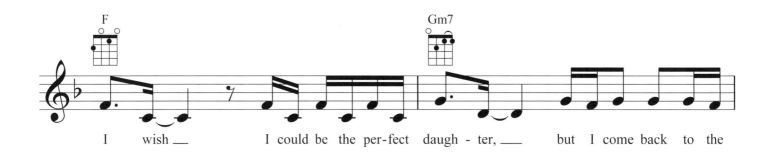

I wish __ I could be the per - fect daugh - ter, __ but I come back to the

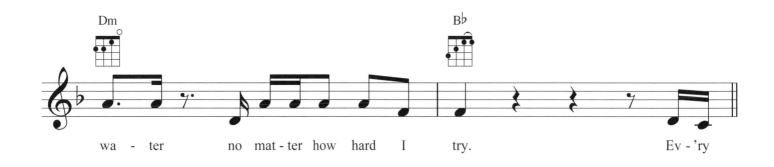

wa - ter no mat - ter how hard I try. Ev - 'ry

Pre-Chorus

Dm ... C

turn I take, ev-'ry trail I track, ev-'ry path I make, ev-'ry road leads back to the

F ... Bbm6

place I know where I can-not go, where I long ___ to be. See the

Chorus

F ... Csus4 ... C

line where the sky meets the sea, it calls ___ me, and no one

Dm ... Bb

knows ___ how far it goes. ___ If the

F ... Csus4 ... C

wind in my sail on the sea stays be-hind ___ me, one day I'll

Dm ... Bbm6

know. ___ If I go, there's just no tell-ing how far I'll

Verse

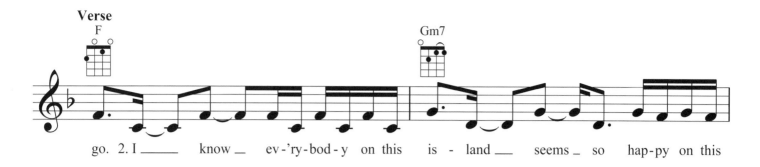

go. 2. I _____ know _____ ev-'ry-bod-y on this is - land _____ seems _ so hap-py on this

is - land. _____ Ev - 'ry - thing is by de - sign. _____

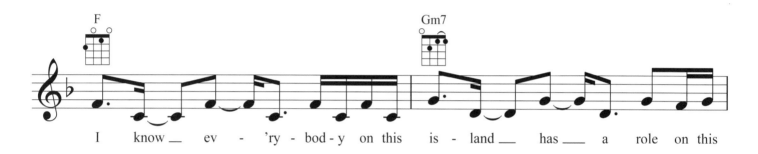

I know _____ ev - 'ry - bod - y on this is - land _____ has _____ a role on this

is - land, _____ so may-be I can roll with mine. _____ I can

Pre-Chorus

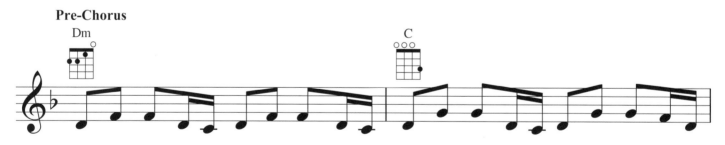

lead with pride, I can make us strong. I'll be sat - is - fied if I play a - long, but the

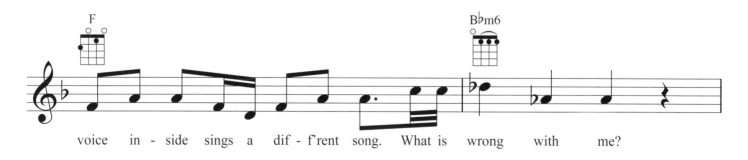

voice in - side sings a dif - f'rent song. What is wrong with me?

How Much Is That Doggie in the Window

Words and Music by Bob Merrill

First note

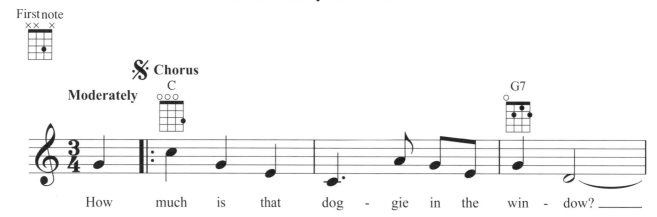

How much is that dog - gie in the win - dow? _____

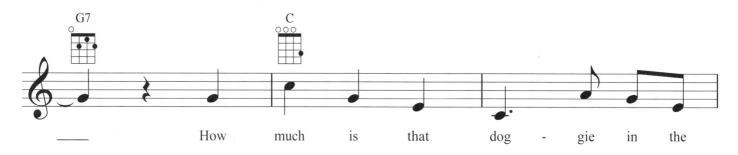

_____ The one with the wag - gl - ey tail. _____

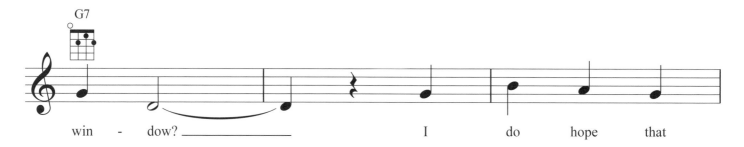

_____ How much is that dog - gie in the

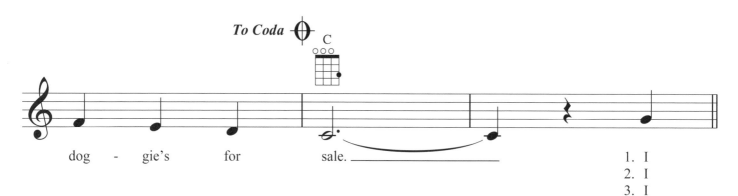

win - dow? _____ I do hope that

dog - gie's for sale. _____
1. I
2. I
3. I

I Just Can't Wait to Be King

from THE LION KING
Music by Elton John
Lyrics by Tim Rice

First note

Verse
Moderately, in 2

Simba: 1. I'm gon-na be a might-y king, so en-e-mies be-

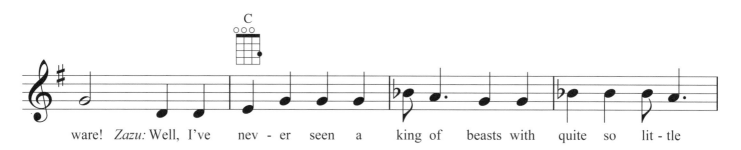

ware! Zazu: Well, I've nev-er seen a king of beasts with quite so lit-tle

hair. Simba: I'm gon-na be the mane e-vent, like no king was be-

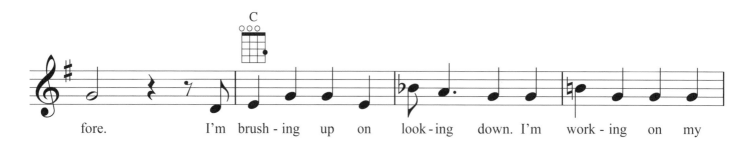

fore. I'm brush-ing up on look-ing down. I'm work-ing on my

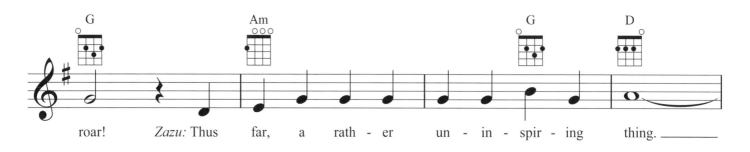

roar! Zazu: Thus far, a rath-er un-in-spir-ing thing. ____

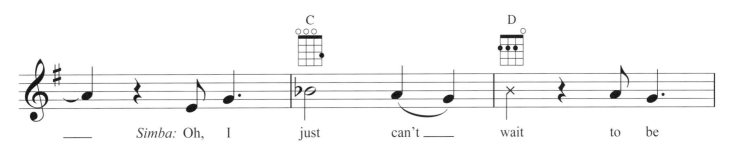

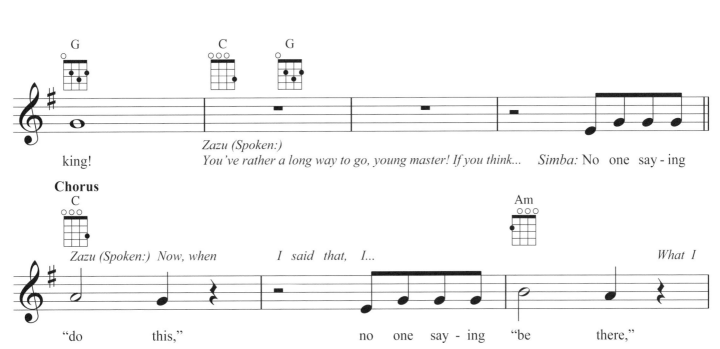

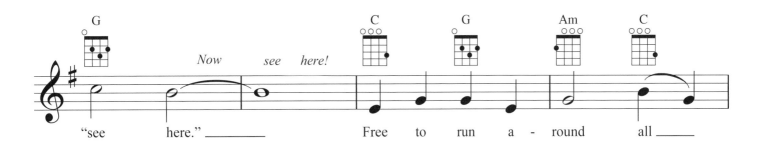

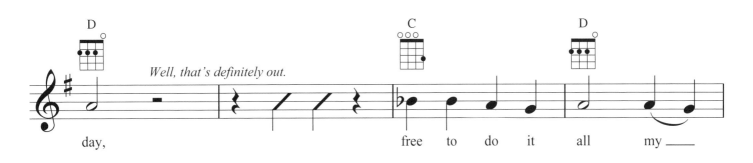

(Quasi spoken:)

way!

Zazu: 2. I

Verse

think it's time that you and I ar - ranged a heart - to -

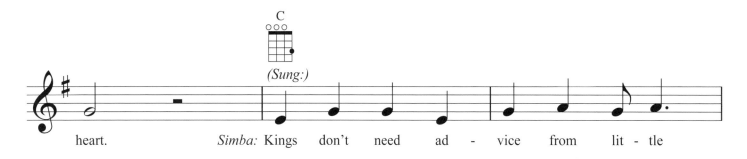

(Sung:)

heart. *Simba:* Kings don't need ad - vice from lit - tle

(Quasi spoken:)

horn - bills, for a start. *Zazu:* If this is where the

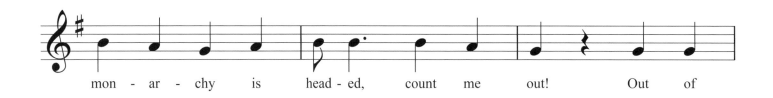

mon - ar - chy is head - ed, count me out! Out of

ser - vice, out of Af - ri - ca. ___ I would - n't hang a -

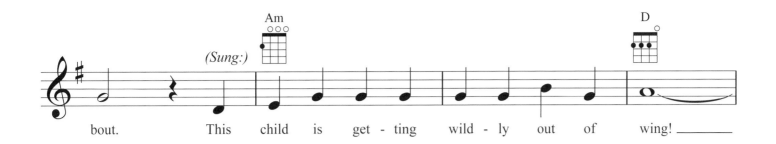

bout.   This   child   is   get - ting   wild - ly   out   of   wing! _____

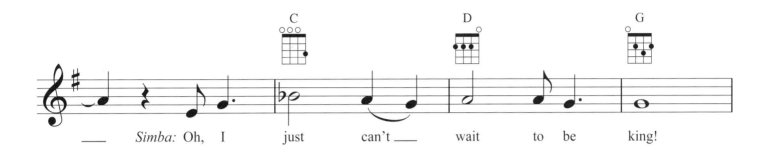

_____   *Simba:* Oh,   I   just   can't _____   wait   to   be   king!

Chorus

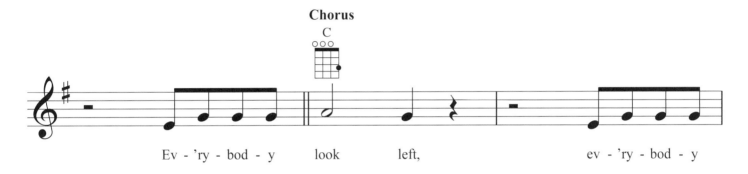

Ev - 'ry - bod - y   look   left,   ev - 'ry - bod - y

look   right.   Ev - 'ry - where you   look   I'm

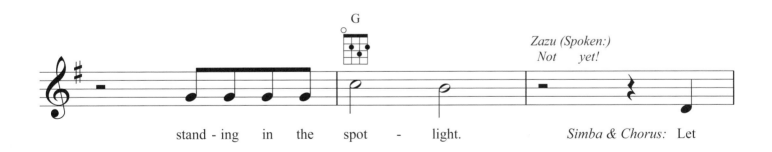

stand - ing   in   the   spot - light.   *Simba & Chorus:* Let

Zazu (Spoken:)
Not   *yet!*

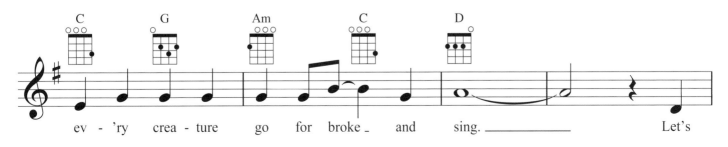

ev - 'ry   crea - ture   go   for   broke _   and   sing. _____   Let's

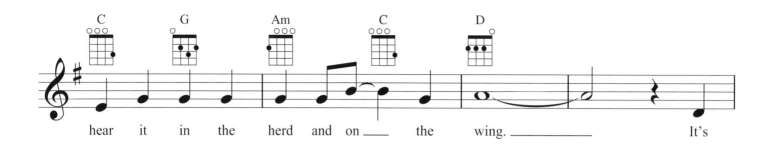

hear it in the herd and on ___ the wing. _____ It's

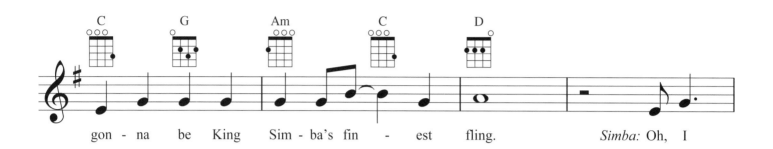

gon - na be King Sim - ba's fin - est fling. *Simba:* Oh, I

just can't ___ wait to be king. Oh, I

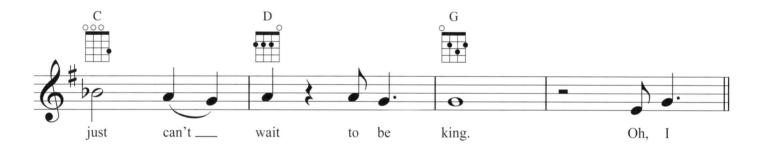

just can't ___ wait to be king. Oh, I

Outro

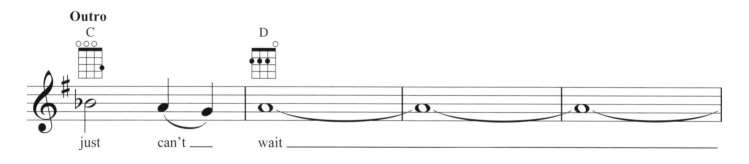

just can't ___ wait _____

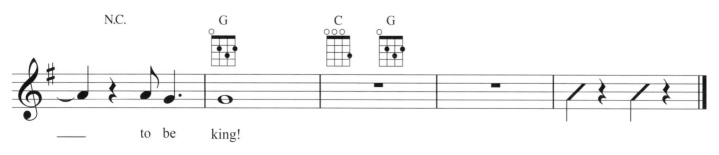

___ to be king!

I Don't Know My Name

Words and Music by Grace VanderWaal

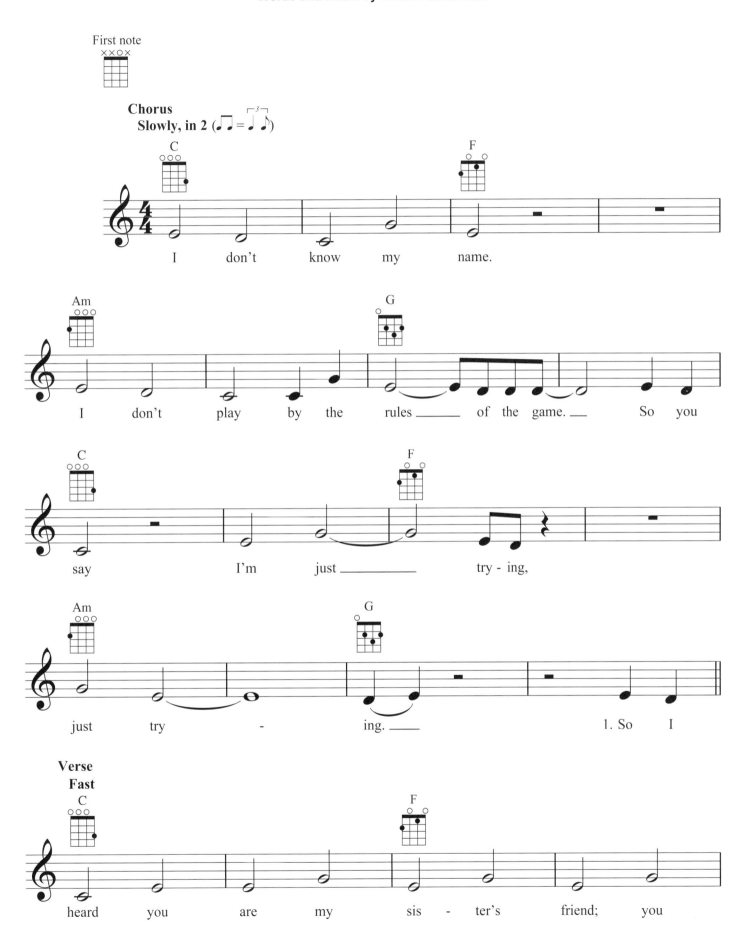

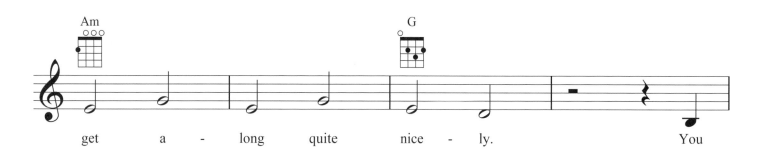

get a - long quite nice - ly. You

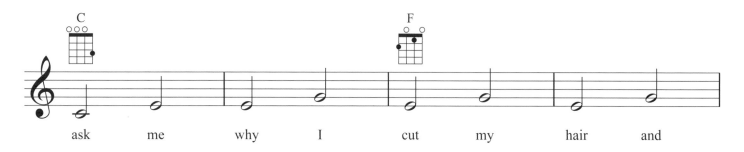

ask me why I cut my hair and

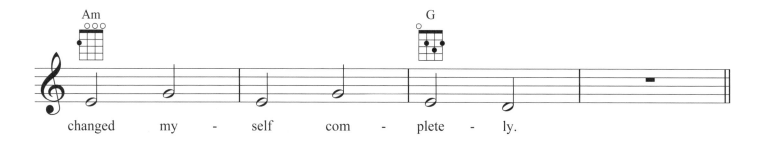

changed my - self com - plete - ly.

𝄋 Chorus
Moderately fast

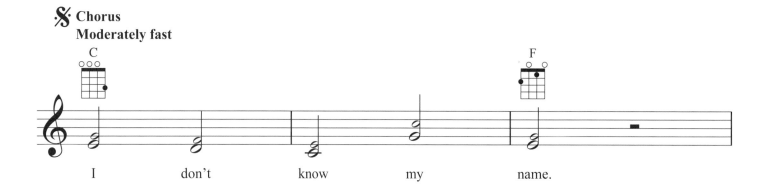

I don't know my name.

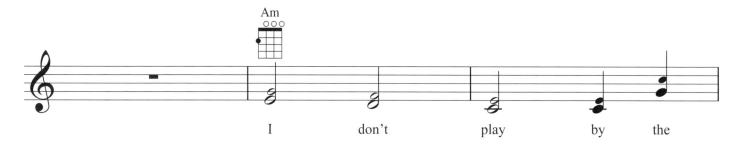

I don't play by the

rules _____ of the game. _____ So you say

Bridge
Freely

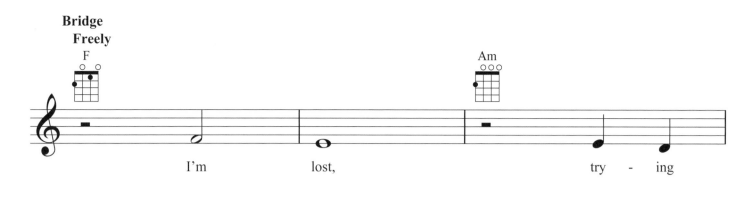

I'm   lost,   try   -   ing

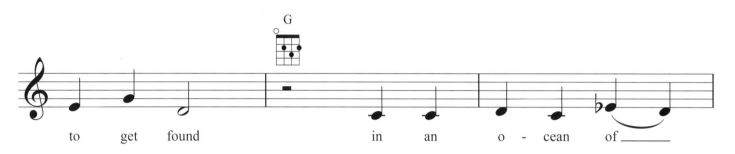

to   get   found   in   an   o - cean   of _____

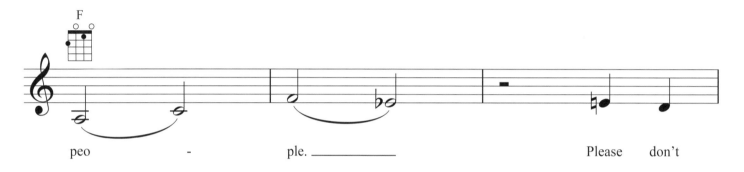

peo   -   ple. _____   Please   don't

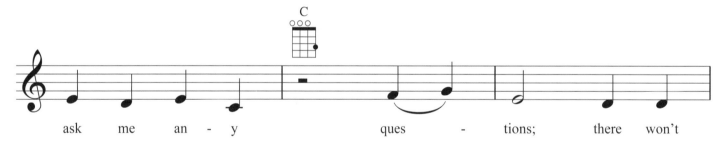

ask   me   an - y   ques - tions;   there   won't

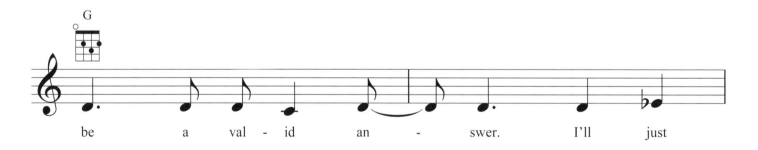

be   a   val - id   an - swer.   I'll   just

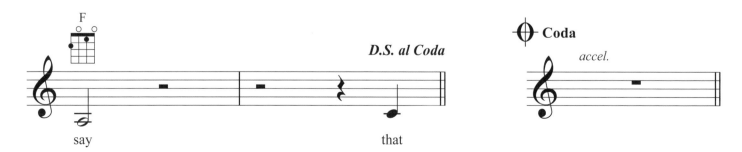

say   that

If You're Happy and You Know It

Words and Music by L. Smith

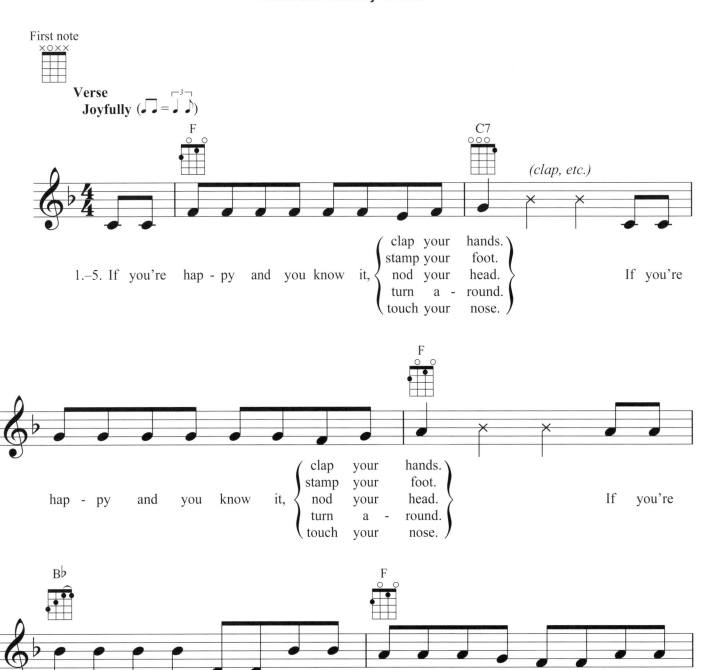

Let's Go Fly a Kite

from MARY POPPINS
Words and Music by Richard M. Sherman and Robert B. Sherman

The More We Get Together

German Folk Song

A Million Dreams

from THE GREATEST SHOWMAN
Words and Music by Benj Pasek and Justin Paul

First note

Verse
Moderately, with intensity

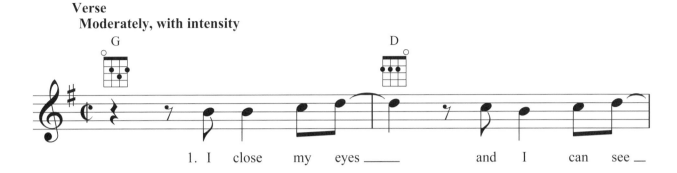

1. I close my eyes _____ and I can see _

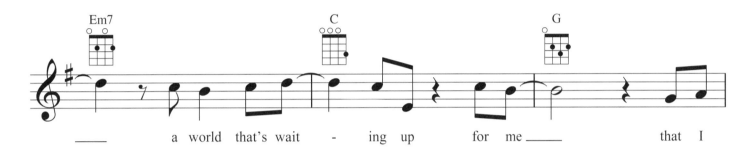

_____ a world that's wait - ing up for me _____ that I

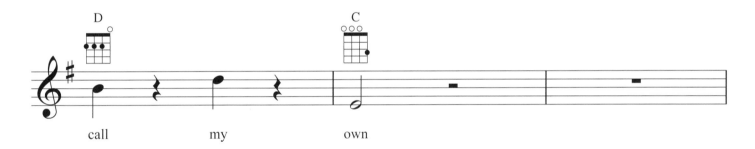

call my own

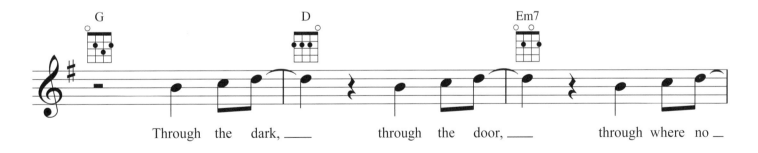

Through the dark, _____ through the door, _____ through where no _

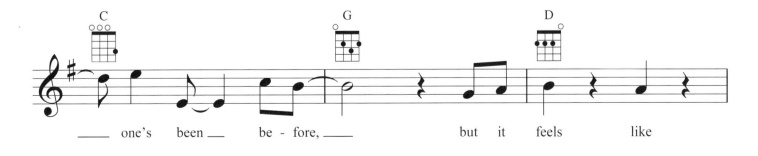

_____ one's been _ be - fore, _____ but it feels like

Interlude

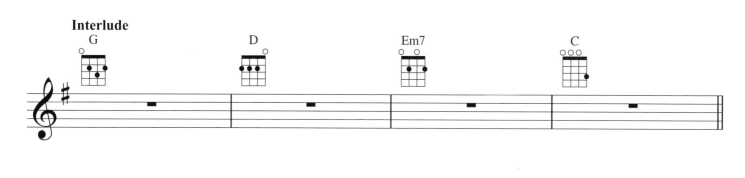

Verse

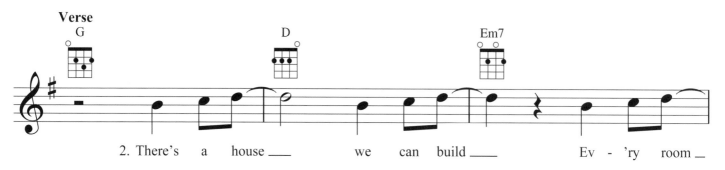

2. There's a house ___ we can build ___ Ev - 'ry room ___

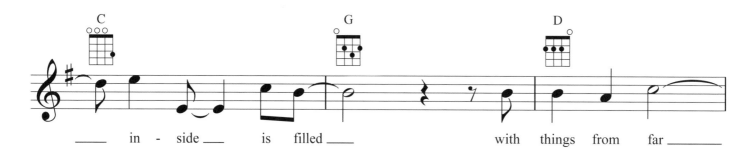

___ in - side ___ is filled ___ with things from far _____

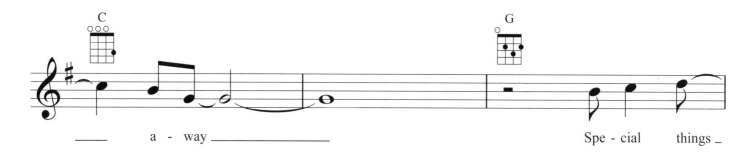

___ a - way _____ Spe - cial things _

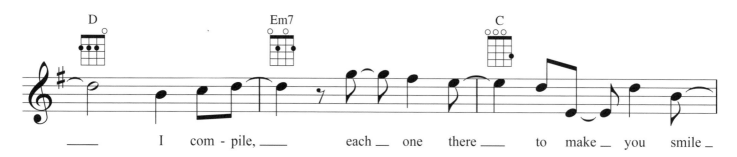

___ I com - pile, ___ each __ one there ___ to make __ you smile _

D.S. al Coda 1

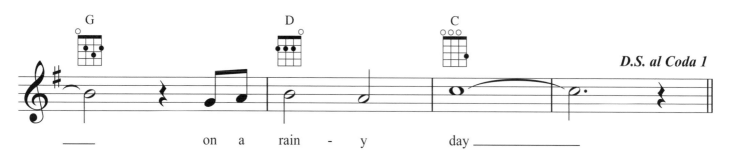

___ on a rain - y day _____

Coda 1

world that we ___ de - sign _____

Chorus

Ev - 'ry night ___ }
ev - 'ry night ___ }
I lie _____ in bed, ___ the

bright - est col - ors fill _____ my ___ head ___ A

mil - lion dreams _____ are keep - in' me ___ a - wake ___

_____ I think of what ___ the world ___

___ could be, ___ a vi - sion of ___ the one ___ I ___ see ___ A

mil - lion dreams __ is all ___ it's gon - na take __

To Coda 2

___ Oh, a mil - lion dreams __ for the world we're gon - na make

Bridge

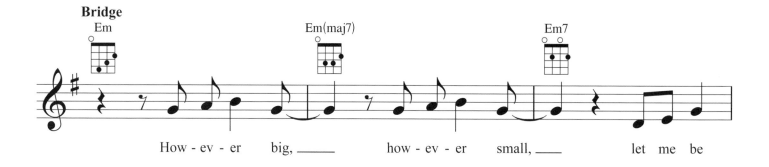

How - ev - er big, ___ how - ev - er small, ___ let me be

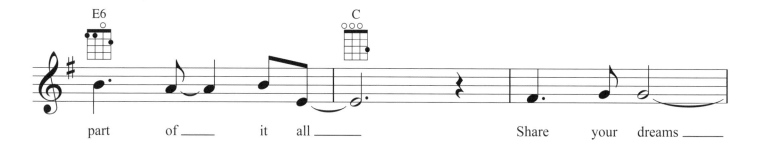

part of ___ it all ___ Share your dreams ___

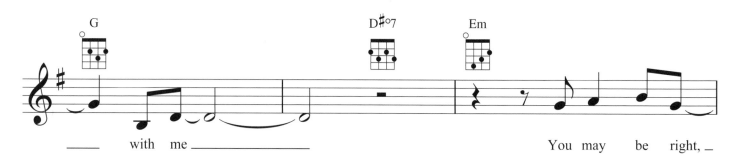

___ with me _____ You may be right, _

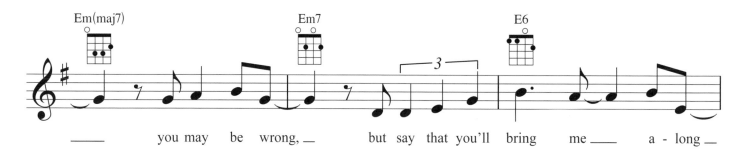

___ you may be wrong, _ but say that you'll bring me ___ a - long _

Naughty

from MATILDA THE MUSICAL
Words and Music by Tim Minchin

Chorus
Moderately fast

Just be-cause you find that life's ___ not fair, ___ it does-n't mean that you just have to grin and bear ___ it. If you al-ways take it on the chin and wear it, noth-ing will change. *(Instrumental)*

E-ven if you're lit-tle, you can do a lot. ___ You must-n't let a lit-tle thing like

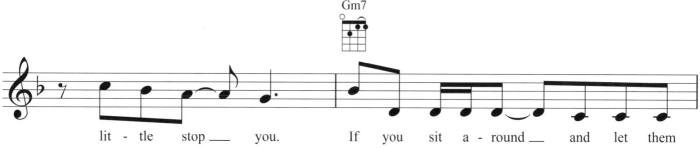

lit-tle stop ___ you. If you sit a-round ___ and let them

get on top, ___ you might as well be say-ing you think that it's o-kay, and that's not right!

And if it's ___ not right, you have to put it right.

Outro

But no-bod-y else ___ is gon-na put it right for me. No-bod-y but me is gon-na change my sto-ry.

Some-times you have to be a lit-tle bit naugh-ty. *(Instrumental)*

Never Smile at a Crocodile

from PETER PAN
Words by Jack Lawrence
Music by Frank Churchill

First note

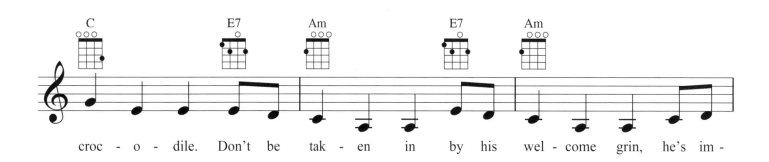

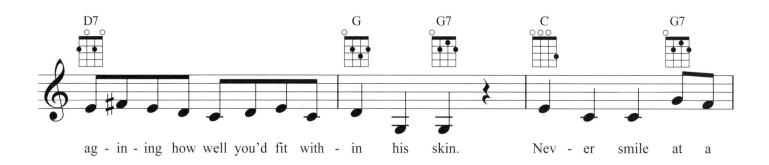

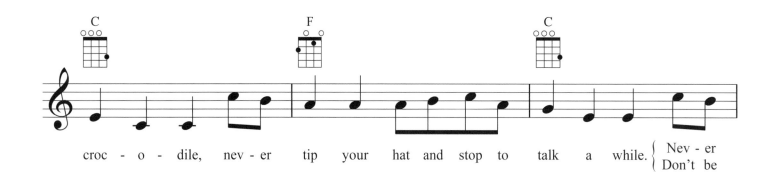

run,   walk a - way,   say "Good - night"   not "Good day!" Clear   the
rude,   nev - er mock,   throw a kiss,   not a rock.

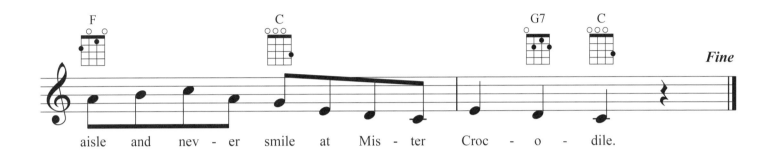

Fine

aisle   and nev - er smile at Mis - ter Croc - o - dile.

Bridge

You may ver - y well be well - bred,   lots of et - i -

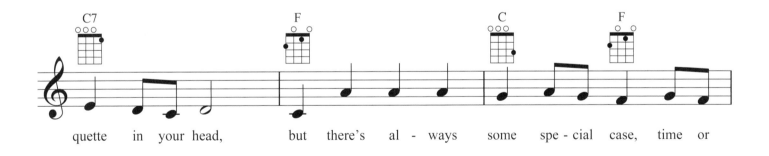

quette in your head,   but there's al - ways some spe - cial case, time or

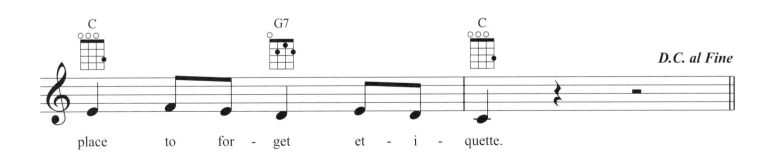

D.C. al Fine

place   to for - get et - i - quette.

Oh Where, Oh Where Has My Little Dog Gone

Words by Sep. Winner
Traditional Melody

First note

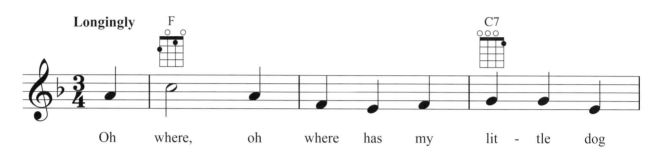

Oh   where,   oh   where   has   my   lit - tle   dog

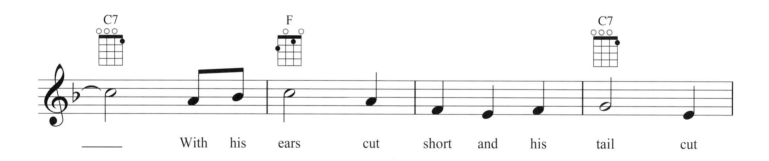

gone?   Oh   where,   oh   where   can   he   be? _____

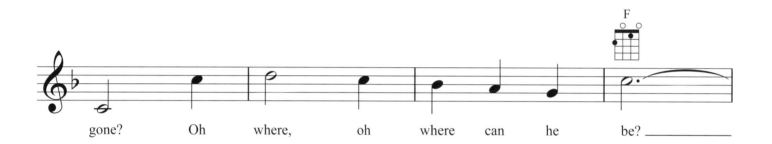

_____   With   his   ears   cut   short   and   his   tail   cut

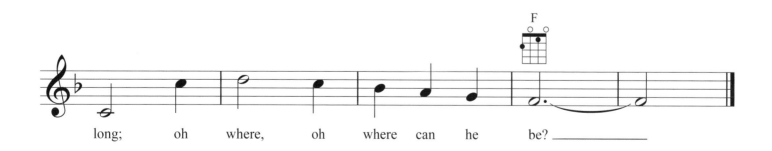

long;   oh   where,   oh   where   can   he   be? _____

Old MacDonald

Traditional Children's Song

First note

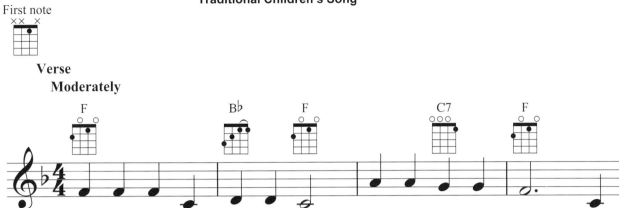

Verse

Moderately

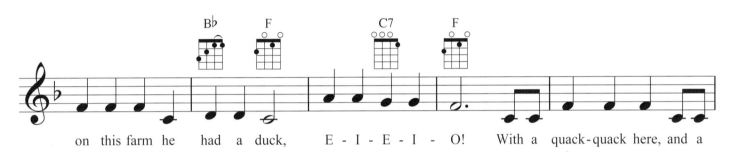

1. Old Mac-Don - ald had a farm, E - I - E - I - O! And
2.–10. *See additional lyrics*

on this farm he had a duck, E - I - E - I - O! With a quack-quack here, and a

quack - quack there, here a quack, there a quack, ev - 'ry - where a quack, quack.

Old Mac-Don - ald had a farm, E - I - E - I - O!

Additional Lyrics

2. Old MacDonald had a farm,
   E-I-E-I-O!
   And on his farm he had a chick,
   E-I-E-I-O!
   With a chick, chick here,
   And a chick, chick there,
   Here a chick, there a chick,
   Everywhere a chick, chick.
   Old MacDonald had a farm,
   E-I-E-I-O!

3. Cow – moo, moo
4. Dog – bow, bow
5. Pig – oink, oink
6. Rooster – cock-a-doodle, cock-a-doodle
7. Turkey – gobble, gobble
8. Cat – meow, meow
9. Horse – neigh, neigh
10. Donkey – hee-haw, hee-haw

On Top of Spaghetti

Words and Music by Tom Glazer

First note

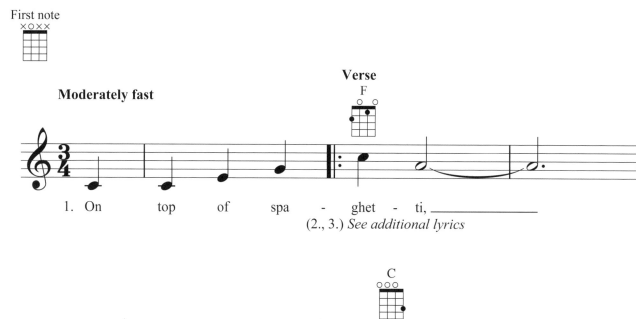

Moderately fast

Verse

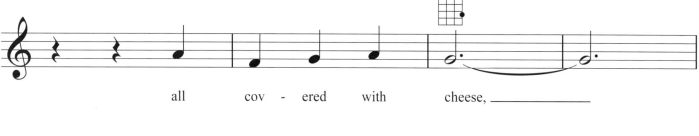

1. On top of spa - ghet - ti, _____
(2., 3.) *See additional lyrics*

all cov - ered with cheese, _____

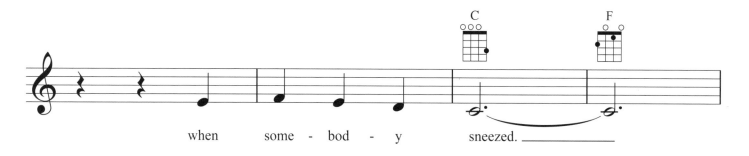

I lost my poor meat - ball _____

when some - bod - y sneezed. _____

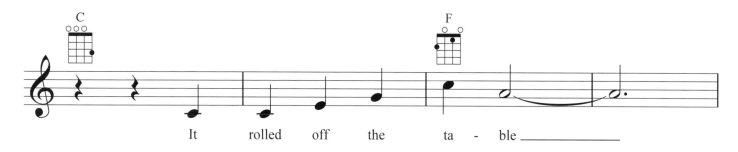

It rolled off the ta - ble _____

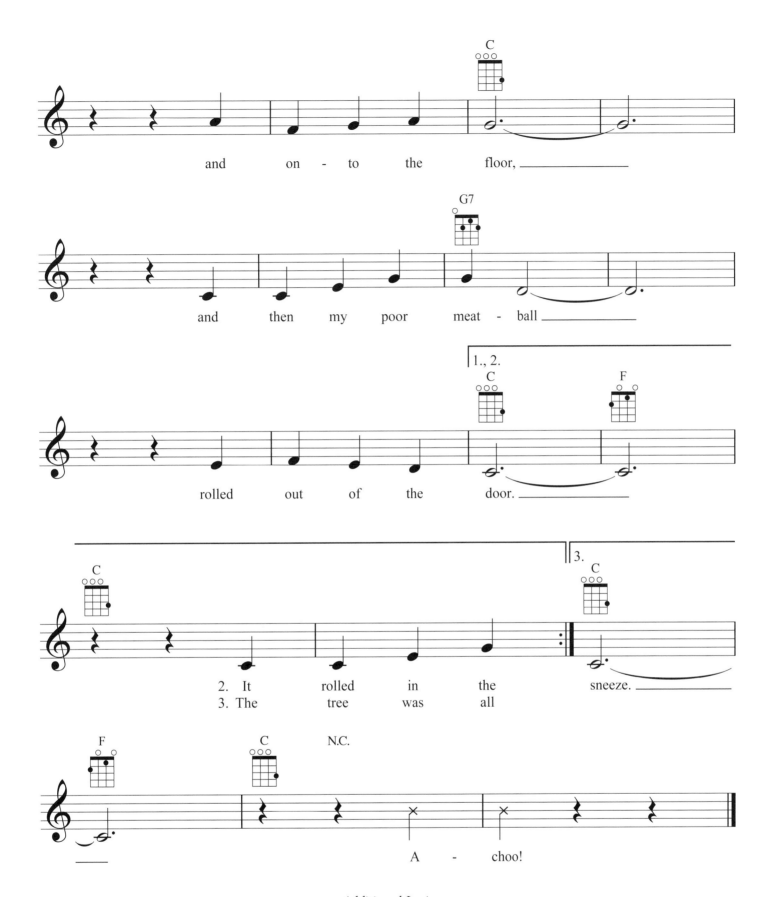

Additional Lyrics

2. It rolled in the garden and under a bush,
   And then my poor meatball was nothing but mush.
   The mush was as tasty as tasty could be,
   And early next summer, it grew into a tree.

3. The tree was all covered with beautiful moss;
   It grew lovely meatballs and tomato sauce.
   So if you eat spaghetti all covered with cheese,
   Hold onto your meatballs and don't ever sneeze.

Row, Row, Row Your Boat

Traditional

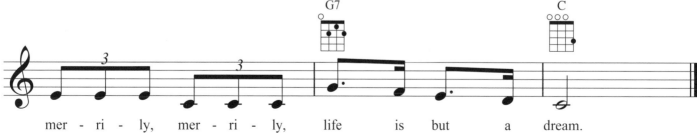

Puff the Magic Dragon

Words and Music by Lenny Lipton and Peter Yarrow

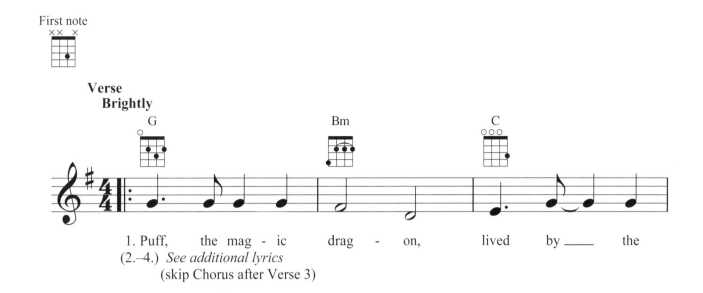

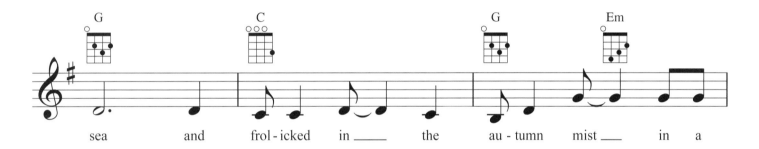

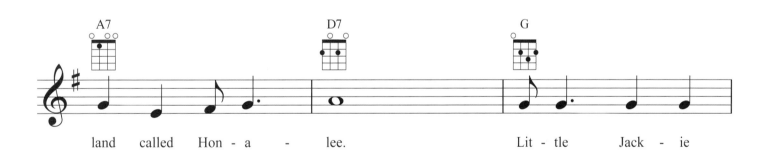

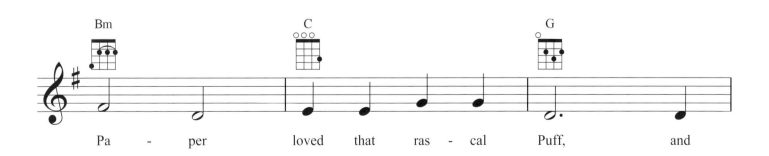

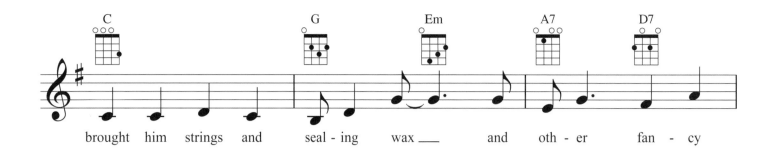

brought him strings and seal - ing wax ___ and oth - er fan - cy

Chorus

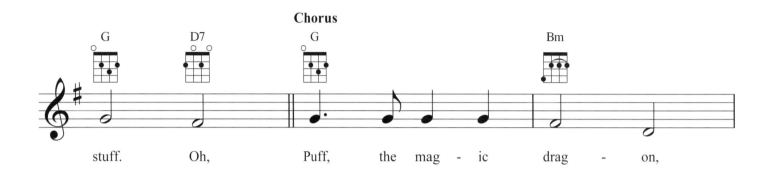

stuff. Oh, Puff, the mag - ic drag - on,

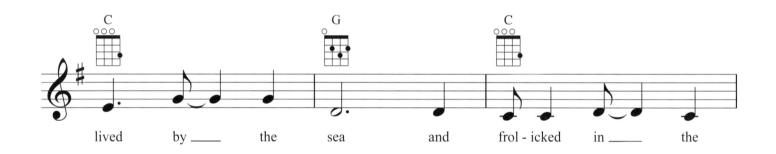

lived by ___ the sea and frol - icked in ___ the

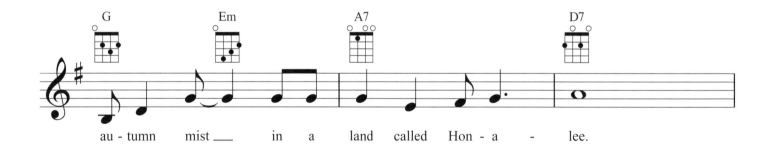

au - tumn mist ___ in a land called Hon - a - lee.

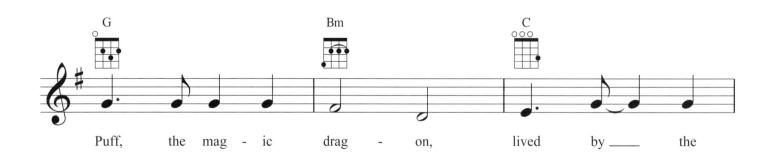

Puff, the mag - ic drag - on, lived by ___ the

sea   and   frol-icked   in ___ the   au-tumn   mist ___ in   a

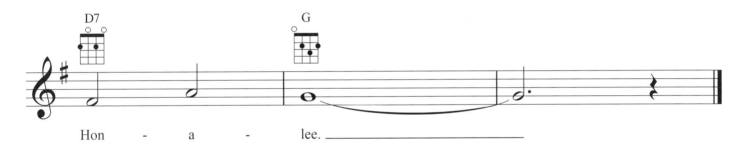

land   called   Hon - a - lee.   2. To - land   called

3. A

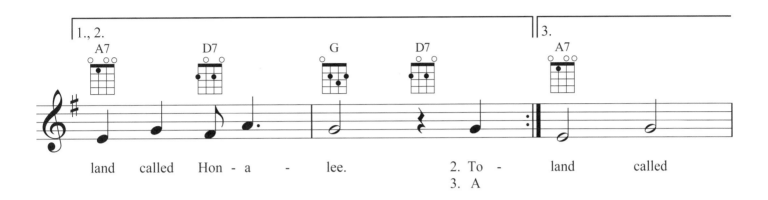

Hon - a - lee. _____

Additional Lyrics

2. Together they would travel on a boat with billowed sail,
   And Jackie kept a lookout perched on Puff's gigantic tail.
   Noble kings and princes would bow whenever they came.
   Pirate ships would lower their flags when Puff roared out his name.

3. A dragon lives forever, but not so little boys.
   Painted wings and giant rings make way for other toys.
   One gray night it happened; Jackie Paper came no more,
   And Puff, that mighty dragon, he ceased his fearless roar. *(To Verse 4)*

4. His head was bent in sorrow, green tears fell like rain.
   Puff no longer went to play along the Cherry Lane.
   Without his lifelong friend, Puff could not be brave.
   So Puff, that mighty dragon, sadly slipped into his cave.

Rubber Duckie

from the Television Series SESAME STREET
Words and Music by Jeff Moss

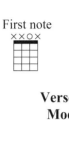

First note

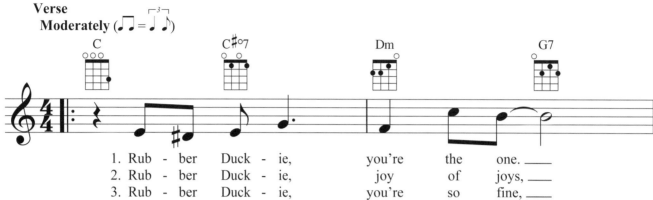

Verse
Moderately

1. Rub - ber Duck - ie, you're the one. ____
2. Rub - ber Duck - ie, joy of joys, ____
3. Rub - ber Duck - ie, you're so fine, ____

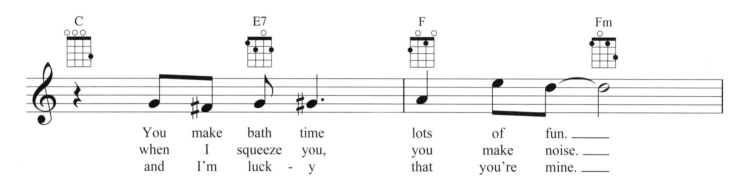

You make bath time lots of fun. ____
when I squeeze you, you make noise. ____
and I'm luck - y that you're mine. ____

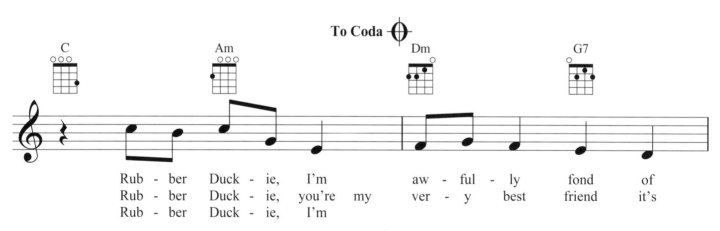

To Coda ⊕

Rub - ber Duck - ie, I'm aw - ful - ly fond of
Rub - ber Duck - ie, you're my ver - y best friend it's
Rub - ber Duck - ie, I'm

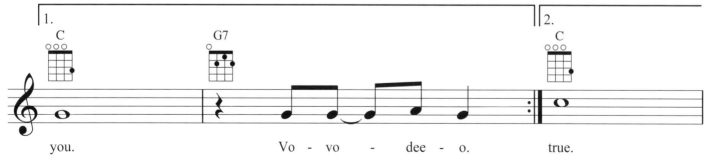

1.
you.   Vo - vo - dee - o.

2.
true.

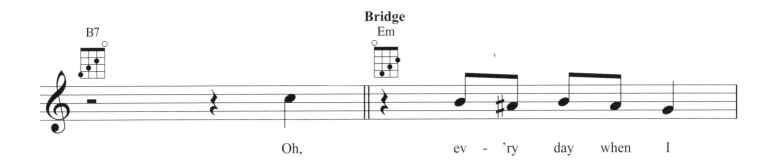

Bridge

Oh, ev - 'ry day when I

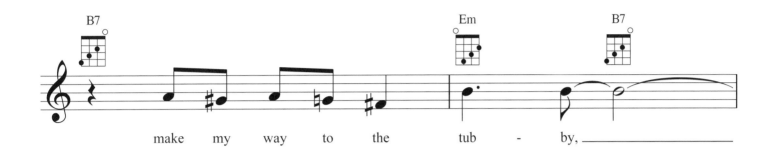

make my way to the tub - by, _____

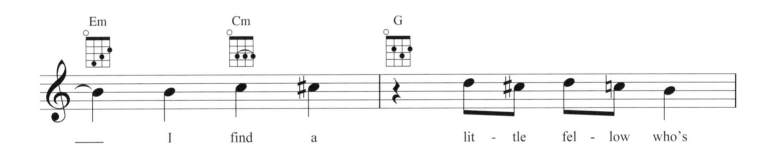

_____ I find a lit - tle fel - low who's

D.C. al Coda

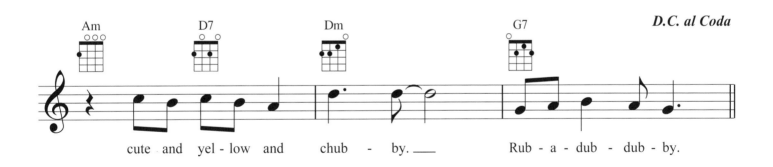

cute and yel - low and chub - by. ___ Rub - a - dub - dub - by.

Coda

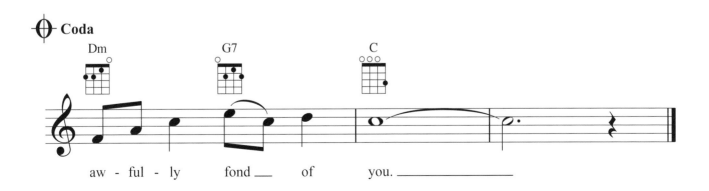

aw - ful - ly fond ___ of you. _____

Sesame Street Theme

from the Television Series SESAME STREET
Words by Bruce Hart, Jon Stone and Joe Raposo
Music by Joe Raposo

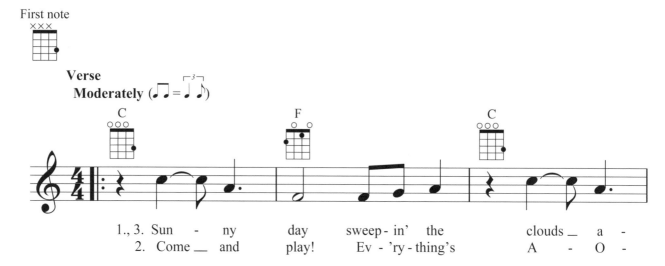

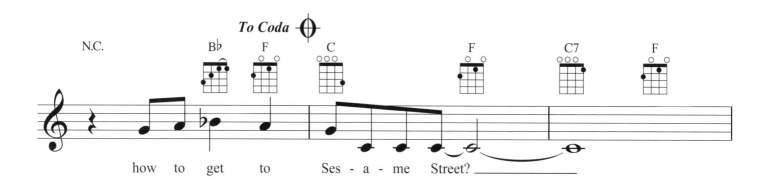

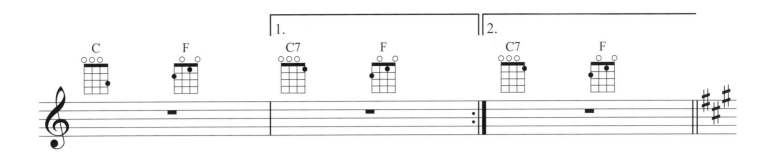

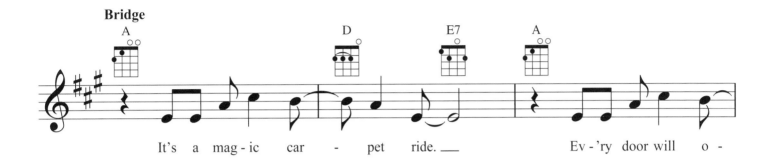

Bridge

It's a mag-ic car - pet ride. ___ Ev -'ry door will o -

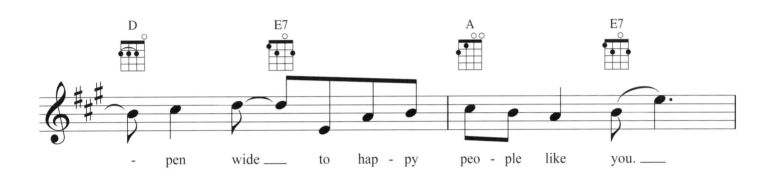

- pen wide ___ to hap - py peo - ple like you. ___

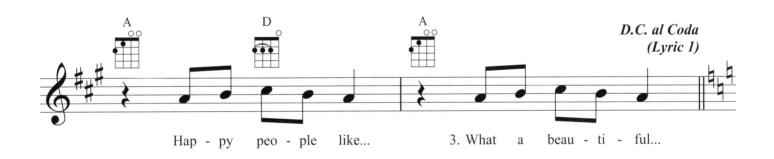

D.C. al Coda
(Lyric 1)

Hap - py peo - ple like... 3. What a beau - ti - ful...

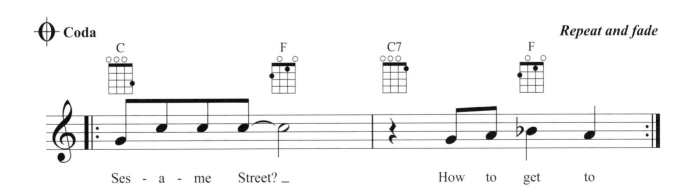

Repeat and fade

Coda

Ses - a - me Street? ___ How to get to

Singin' in the Rain

from SINGIN' IN THE RAIN

Lyric by Arthur Freed
Music by Nacio Herb Brown

First note

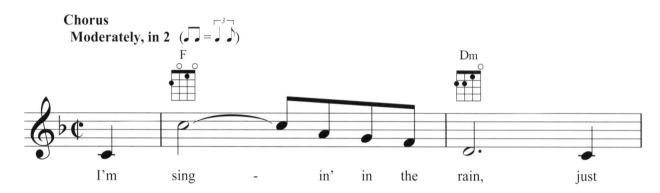

I'm sing - in' in the rain, just

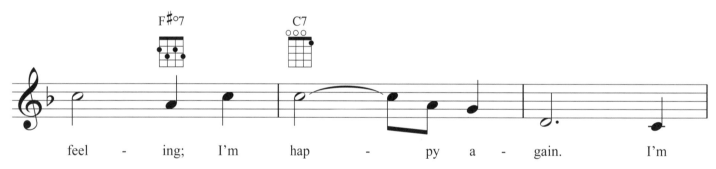

sing - in' in the rain. What a glo - ri - ous

feel - ing; I'm hap - py a - gain. I'm

laugh - ing at clouds so dark up a -

bove. The sun's _____ in my heart _____ and I'm

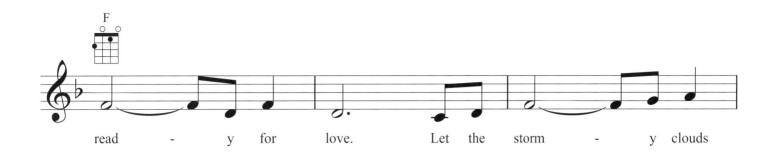

read - y for love. Let the storm - y clouds

chase ev - 'ry - one _____ from the place. Come

on _____ with the rain; I've a smile _____ on my

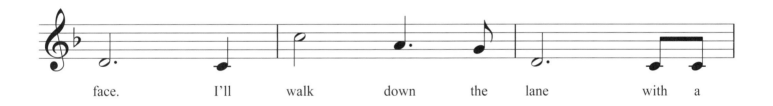

face. I'll walk down the lane with a

hap - py re - frain, and sing - in', _____ just

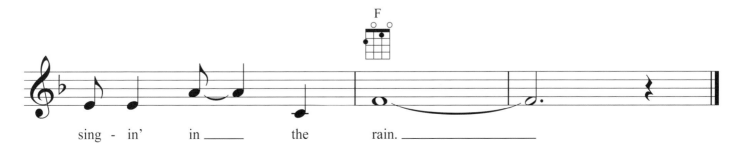

sing - in' in _____ the rain. _____

Somewhere Out There

from AN AMERICAN TAIL

Music by Barry Mann and James Horner
Lyric by Cynthia Weil

far a-part we are, it helps to think we might be wish-in'

on the same bright star. And when the night wind starts to sing that

lone-some ___ lull-a-by, it helps to think we're sleep-ing un-der-

Outro-Verse

neath the same big sky. Some-where out there, if

love can see us through, then we'll be to-geth-er some-where

out there, out where dreams come true. ___

SpongeBob SquarePants Theme Song

from SPONGEBOB SQUAREPANTS

**Words and Music by Mark Harrison, Blaise Smith,
Steve M. Hillenburg and Derek Drymon**

First note

Chorus
Moderately

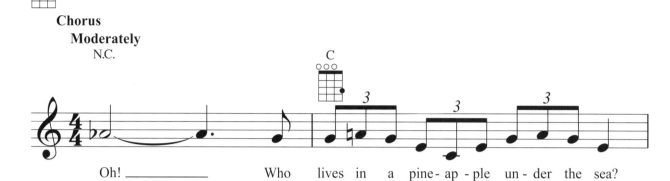

Oh! _____ Who lives in a pine-ap-ple un-der the sea?

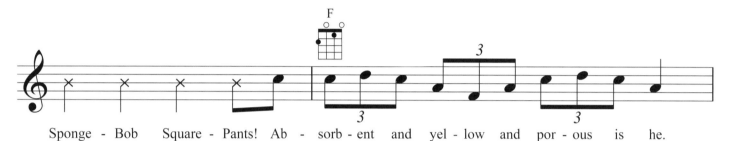

Sponge - Bob Square - Pants! Ab - sorb - ent and yel - low and por - ous is he.

Sponge - Bob Square - Pants! If nau - ti - cal non - sense be some - thing you wish,

Sponge - Bob Square - Pants! then drop on the deck and flop like a fish! Sponge - Bob Square - Pants!

Sponge - Bob Square - Pants! Sponge - Bob Square - Pants! Sponge - Bob Square - Pants! Sponge - Bob Square -

Pants! *(Instrumental)*

Supercalifragilisticexpialidocious

from MARY POPPINS

Words and Music by Richard M. Sherman and Robert B. Sherman

First note

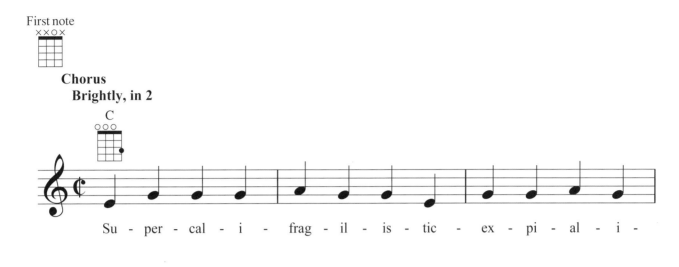

Su - per - cal - i - frag - il - is - tic - ex - pi - al - i -

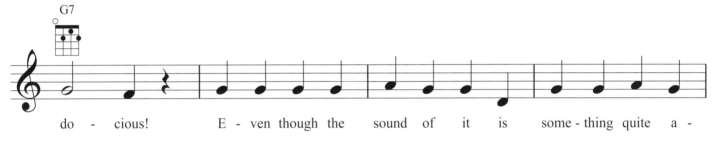

do - cious! E - ven though the sound of it is some - thing quite a -

tro - cious, if you say it loud e - nough, you'll

al - ways sound pre - co - cious. Su - per - cal - i -

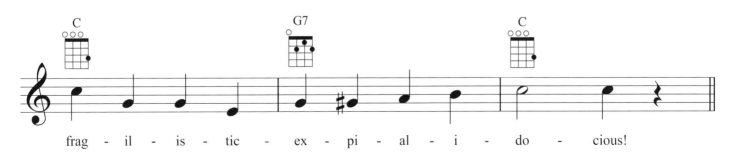

frag - il - is - tic - ex - pi - al - i - do - cious!

Interlude

Um did-dle did-dle did-dle, um did-dle ay! Um did-dle did-dle did-dle,

Verse

um did-dle ay!

1. Be - cause I was a - fraid to speak when
2. He trav - eled all a - round the world and
3. So when the cat has got your tongue, there's

I was just a lad, me fa - ther gave me
ev - 'ry - where he went he'd use his word and
no need for dis - may. Just sum - mon up this

nose a tweak and told me I was bad. But
all would say, "There goes a clev - er gent!" When
word and then you've got a lot to say. But

then one day I learned a word that saved me ach - in'
dukes and ma - 'a - ra - jas pass the time of day with
bet - ter use it care - ful - ly or it can change your

nose, the big - gest word you ev - er 'eard and
me, I say me word spe - cial word and then they
life. One night I said it to me girl and

84

A Spoonful of Sugar

from MARY POPPINS
Words and Music by Richard M. Sherman and Robert B. Sherman

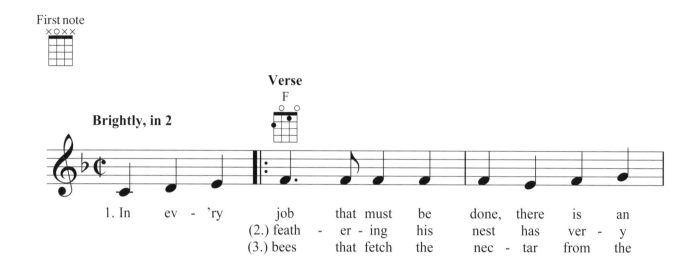

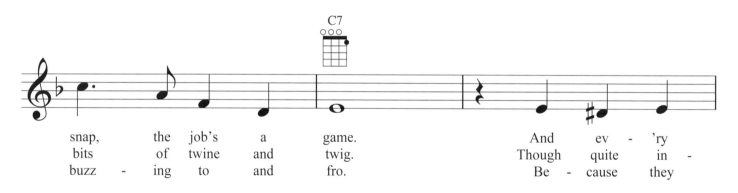

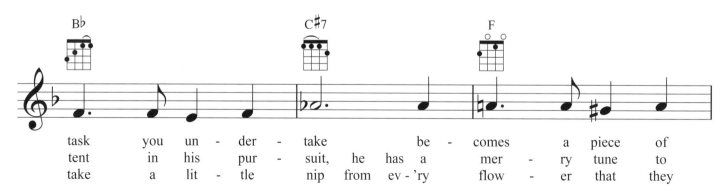

Take Me Out to the Ball Game

from TAKE ME OUT TO THE BALL GAME

Words by Jack Norworth
Music by Albert von Tilzer

First note

Brightly

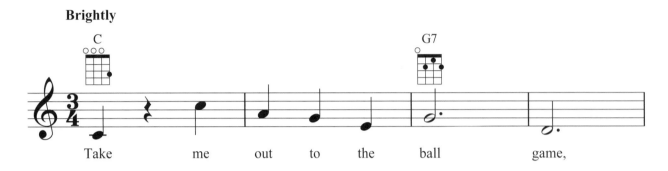

Take me out to the ball game,

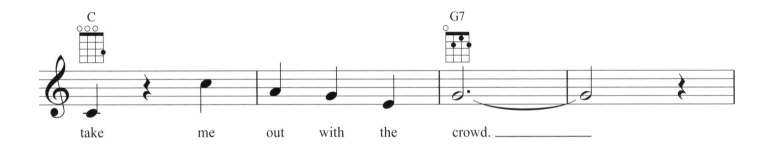

take me out with the crowd. _____

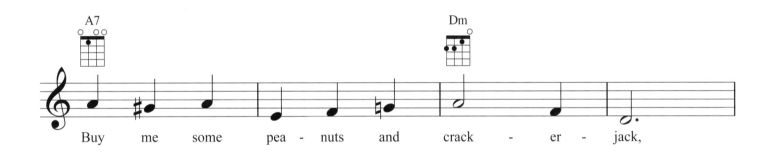

Buy me some pea - nuts and crack - er - jack,

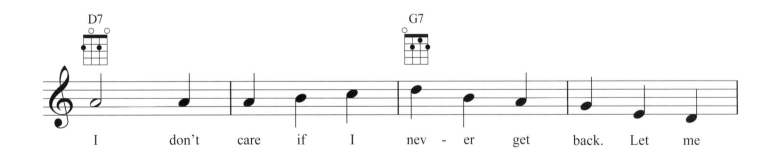

I don't care if I nev - er get back. Let me

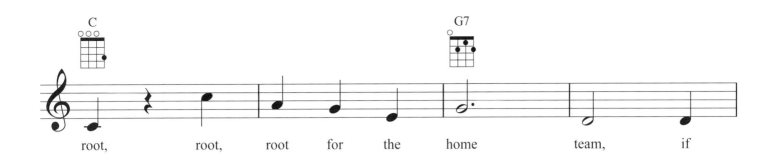

root,   root,   root   for   the   home   team,   if

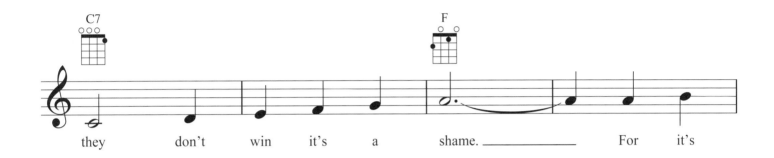

they   don't   win   it's   a   shame. _____   For   it's

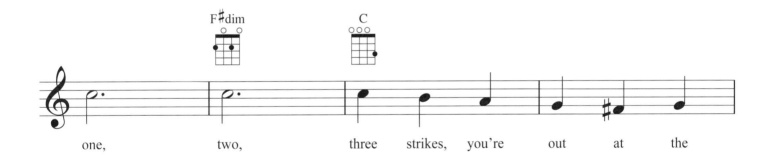

one,   two,   three strikes, you're   out   at   the

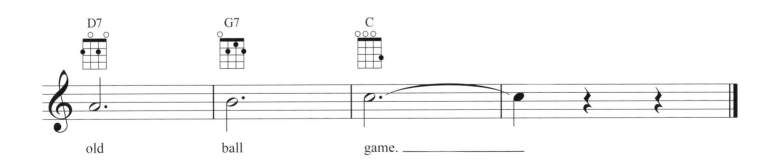

old   ball   game. _____

This Old Man

Traditional

First note

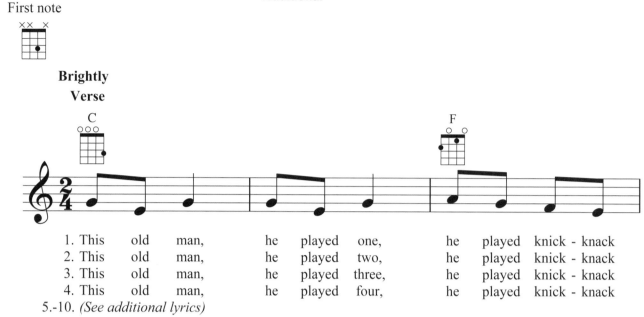

Brightly

Verse

1. This old man, he played one, he played knick-knack
2. This old man, he played two, he played knick-knack
3. This old man, he played three, he played knick-knack
4. This old man, he played four, he played knick-knack

5.-10. *(See additional lyrics)*

Refrain

on my drum.
on my shoe.
on my knee.
on my door.

With a knick-knack pad-dy-whack, give the dog a bone, this old man came roll-ing home.

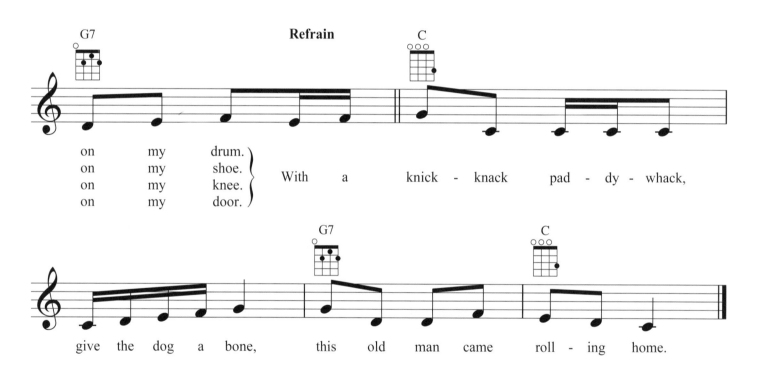

Additional Lyrics

5. This old man, he played five,
   He played knick-knack on my hive.
   Refrain

6. This old man, he played six,
   He played knick-knack on my sticks.
   Refrain

7. This old man, he played seven,
   He played knick-knack up to heaven.
   Refrain

8. This old man, he played eight,
   He played knick-knack at the gate.
   Refrain

9. This old man, he played nine,
   He played knick-knack on my line.
   Refrain

10. This old man, he played ten,
    He played knick-knack over again.
    Refrain

Twinkle, Twinkle Little Star

Traditional

Twin - kle, twin - kle, lit - tle star; how I won - der what you are. Up a - bove the world so high, like a dia - mond in the sky! Twin - kle, twin - kle, lit - tle star; how I won - der what you are.

Tomorrow

from the Musical Production ANNIE
Lyric by Martin Charnin
Music by Charles Strouse

First note

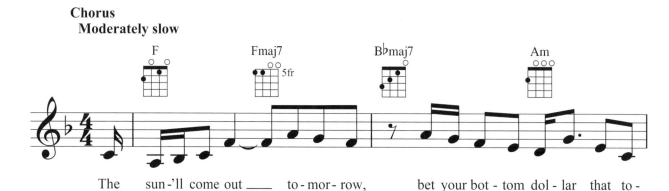

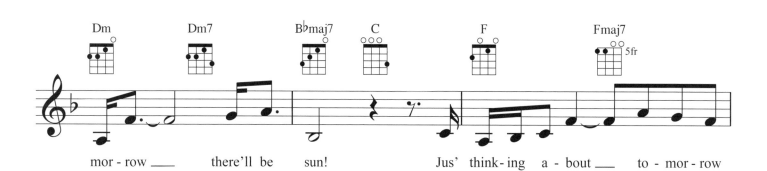

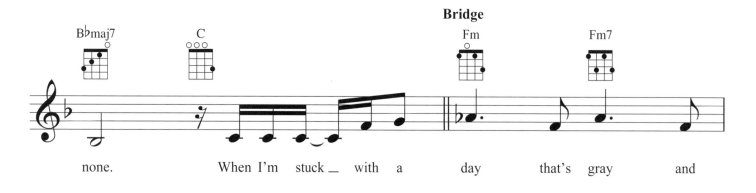

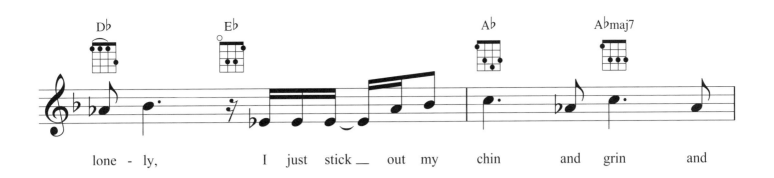

lone - ly,   I   just   stick   out   my   chin   and   grin   and

Chorus

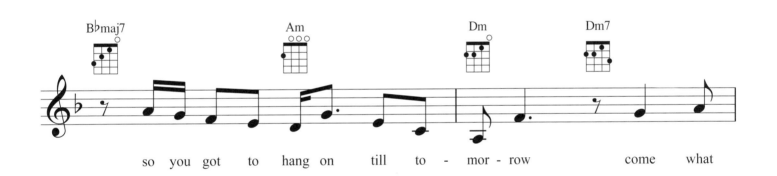

say: _____   Oh!   the   sun -'ll   come   out ____   to - mor - row,

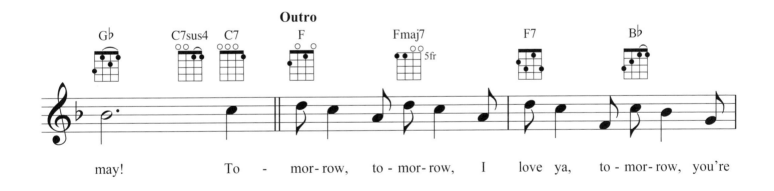

so   you   got   to   hang   on   till   to - mor - row   come   what

Outro

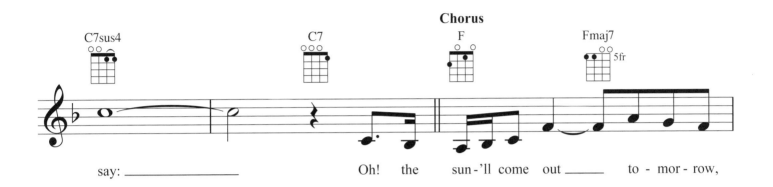

may!   To - mor- row,   to - mor- row,   I   love   ya,   to - mor- row,   you're

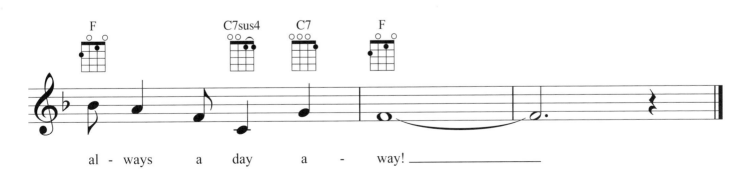

al - ways   a   day   a - way! _____

Un Poco Loco

from COCO
Music by Germaine Franco
Lyrics by Adrian Molina

First note

Verse
Moderately, in 2, with a bounce

MIGUEL:

1. What col - or is the sky? Ay mi a - mor, ___ ay mi a - mor. ___

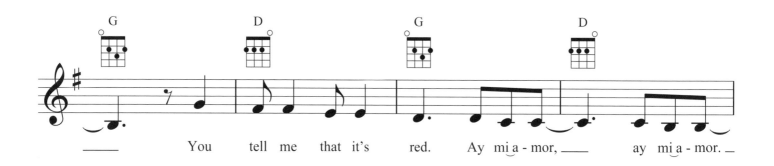

___ You tell me that it's red. Ay mi a - mor, ___ ay mi a - mor. ___

___ Where should I put my shoes? Ay mi a - mor, ___ ay mi a - mor.

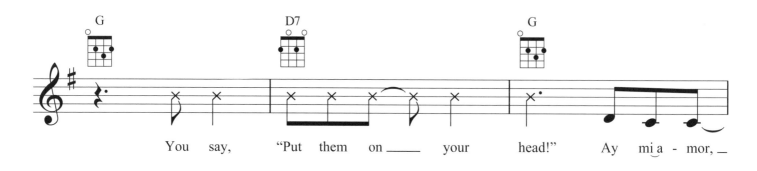

You say, "Put them on ___ your head!" Ay mi a - mor,

Chorus 1

Interlude

Play 6 times

HÉCTOR:

2. The lo - co that you make ___

Verse

___ me, it is just un ___ po - co cra - zy. ___ The

sense that you're not mak - ing, ___ (the **MIGUEL:** lib - er - ties ___ you're

MIGUEL & HÉCTOR:

tak - ing,) ___ leaves my ca - be - za shak - ing. ___

AUDIENCE:

___ You are just un po - co lo - co. ___ He's

Chorus 2

just un po - co cra - zy, ___ leaves my ca - be - za

shak - ing. ___ He's just un po - co cra - zy, ___ leaves my ca - be - za

shak - ing. ___ He's just un po - co cra - zy, ___ leaves my ca - be - za

shak - ing. ___ He's just un po - co cra - zy, ___ leaves my ca - be - za

Outro

shak - ing. ___ **HÉCTOR:** (Un po - qui - ti - ti - ti - ti - ti - ti - ti -
MIGUEL: Un po - qui - ti - ti - ti - ti - ti - ti -

ti - ti - ti - ti - ti - ti - ti - ti - ti - ti - ti - ti - to lo - co.) ___
ti - ti - ti - ti - ti - ti - ti - ti - to lo - co. ___

Warm Kitty

Music adapted from an English Folk Tune by Laura Pendleton MacCarteney
Lyrics by Edith Newlin

First note

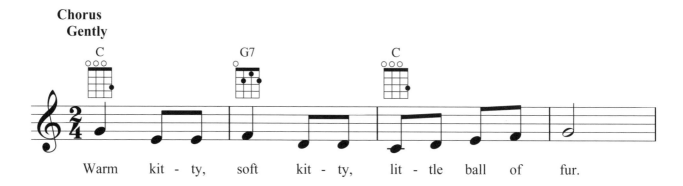

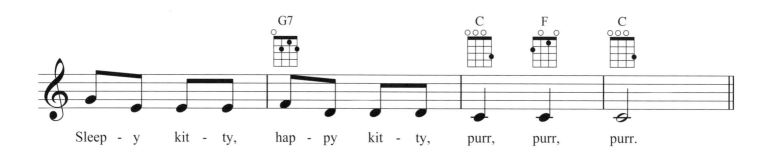

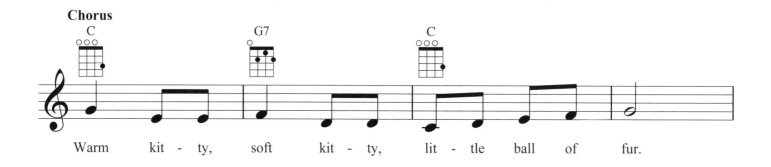

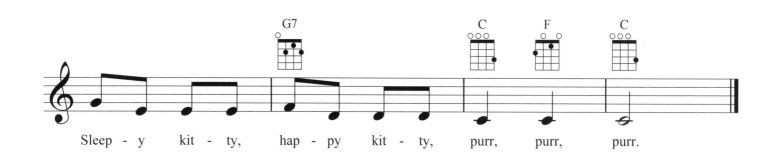

The Unicorn

Words and Music by Shel Silverstein

First note

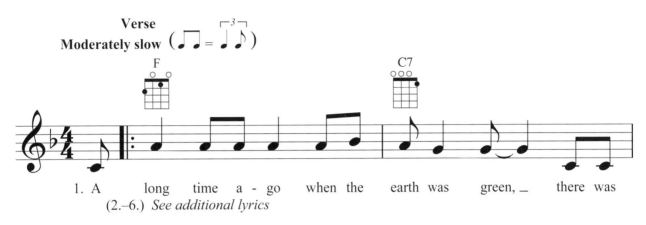

1. A long time a-go when the earth was green, _ there was
(2.–6.) *See additional lyrics*

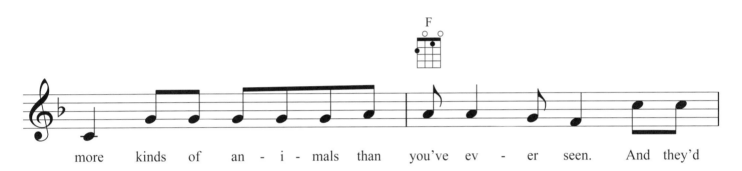

more kinds of an - i - mals than you've ev - er seen. And they'd

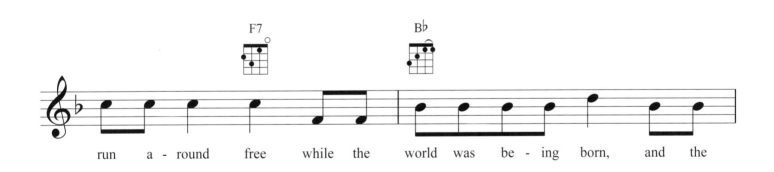

run a - round free while the world was be - ing born, and the

love - li - est of all was the u - ni - corn. There was

Chorus

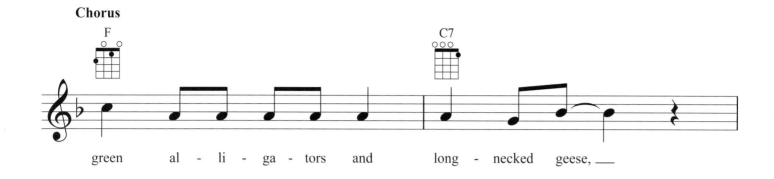

green al - li - ga - tors and long - necked geese, ___

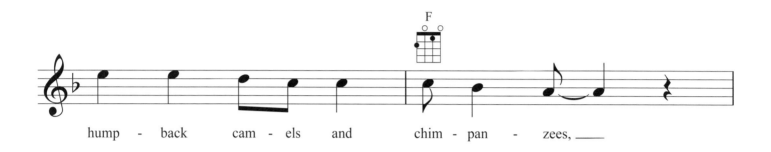

hump - back cam - els and chim - pan - zees, ___

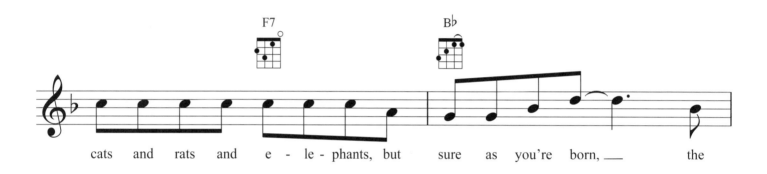

cats and rats and e - le - phants, but sure as you're born, ___ the

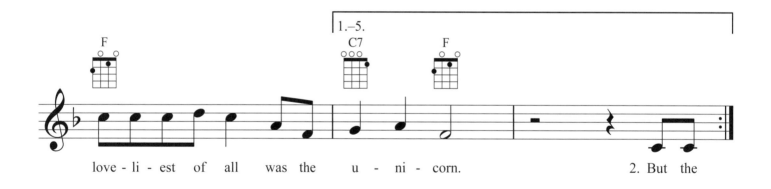

love - li - est of all was the u - ni - corn.   2. But the

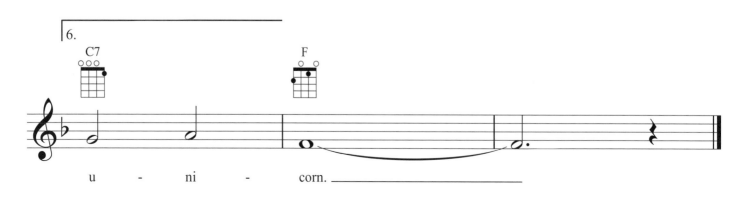

u - ni - corn. _____

The Unicorn

(Additional Lyrics)

2. But the Lord seen some sinnin' and it caused him pain.
   He says, "Stand back, I'm gonna make it rain.
   So, hey, Brother Noah, I'll tell you what to do,
   Go and build me a floating zoo."
Chorus: "Two alligators and a couple of geese,
   Two hump-back camels and two chimpanzees,
   Two cats, two rats, two elephants, but sure as you're born,
   Noah, don't you forget my unicorns."

3. Now Noah was there and he answered the callin'
   And he finished up the ark as the rain started fallin'.
   Then he marched in the animals two by two,
   And he sung out as they went through:
Chorus: "Hey, Lord, I got you two alligators and a couple of geese,
   Two hump-back camels and two chimpanzees,
   Two cats, two rats, two elephants, but sure as you're born,
   Lord, I don't see your unicorns."

4. Well, Noah looked out through the drivin' rain,
   But the unicorns was hidin' — playin' silly games.
   They were kickin' and a-spashin' while the rain was pourin',
   Oh, them foolish unicorns.
Chorus: "Hey, Lord, I got you two alligators and a couple of geese,
   Two hump-back camels and two chimpanzees,
   Two cats, two rats, two elephants, but sure as you're born,
   Lord, I don't see your unicorns."

5. Then the ducks started duckin' and the snakes started snakin',
   And the elephants started elephantin' and the boat started shakin',
   The mice started squeakin' and the lions started roarin',
   And everyone's aboard but them unicorns.
Chorus: I mean the two alligators and a couple of geese,
   The hump-back camels and the chimpanzees,
   Noah cried, "Close the door 'cause the rain is pourin',
   And we just can't wait for them unicorns."

6. And then the ark started movin' and it drifted with the tide
   And the unicorns looked up from the rock and cried,
   And the water came up and sort of floated them away.
   That's why you've never seen a unicorn to this day.
Chorus: You'll see a lot of alligators and a whole mess of geese,
   You'll see hump-back camels and chimpanzees,
   You'll see cats and rats and elephants, but sure as you're born,
   You're never gonna see no unicorn.

When I Grow Up

from MATILDA THE MUSICAL
Words and Music by Tim Minchin

First note

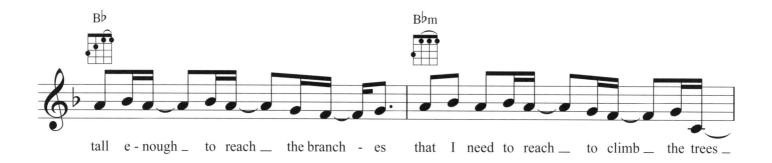

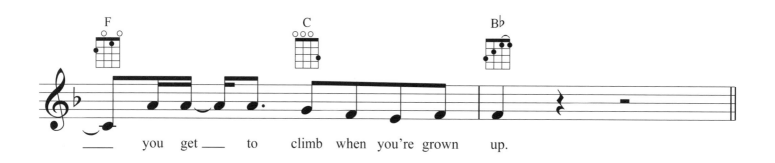

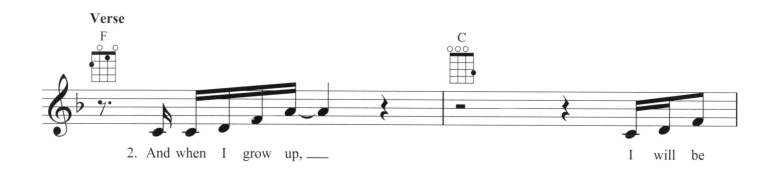

smart e - nough __ to an - swer all ___ the ques - tions that you need __ to know __ the an -

- swers to be - fore you're grown up. _____

Chorus

And when I grow up, ___ I will eat sweets ev - 'ry day ___ on the way __

___ to work __ and I ___ will go to bed ___ late ev - 'ry night. __

And I will wake up ___ when the sun ___ comes up and I ___ will watch car -

toons un - til my eyes __ go square __ and I won't care 'cause I'll __ be all ___ grown up __

when I ___ grow up.

Verse

3. When I grow up, ___ (when I grow up. when I grow up,) I will be

strong e - nough ___ to car - ry all ___ the heav - y things ___ you have ___ to haul ___ a - round ___

___ with you ___ when you're a grown up. ___

Verse

4. And when I grow up, ___ (when I grow up, when I grow up,) I will be

brave e - nough ___ to fight ___ the crea - tures that you have to fight ___ be - neath ___ the bed

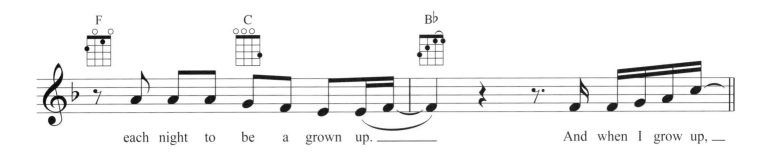

each night to be a grown up. _____ And when I grow up, __

Outro-Chorus

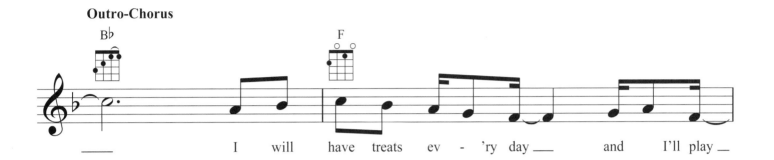

____ I will have treats ev - 'ry day __ and I'll play __

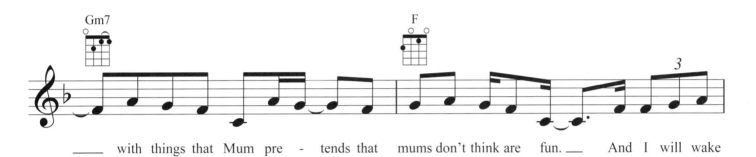

____ with things that Mum pre - tends that mums don't think are fun. __ And I will wake

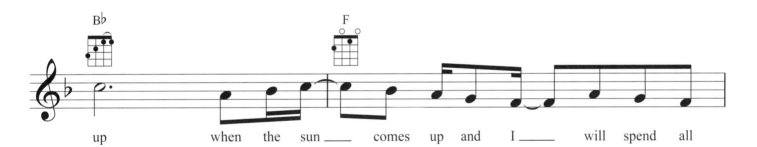

up when the sun ___ comes up and I ____ will spend all

day just ly - ing in ___ the sun ___ and I won't burn 'cause I'll __ be all ___ grown up __

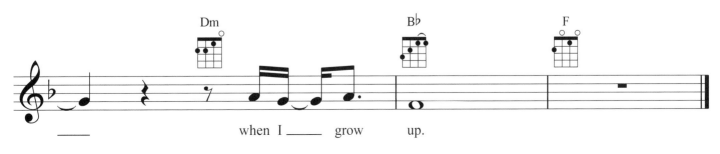

____ when I ___ grow up.

You Are My Sunshine

Words and Music by Jimmie Davis

_____ my on - ly sun - shine, _____ you make me

hap - py _____ when skies are gray. _____

_____ You'll nev - er know, dear, _____ how much I

love you. _____ Please don't take my sun - shine a -

way. _____ 2. I'll al - ways way. _____
3. You told me

Additional Lyrics

2. I'll always love you and make you happy
   If you will only say the same.
   But if you leave me to love another,
   You'll regret it all someday.

3. You told me once, dear, you really loved me
   And no one else could come between.
   But now you've left me and love another;
   You have shattered all my dreams.

The Wheels on the Bus

Traditional

First note

Verse

Moderately

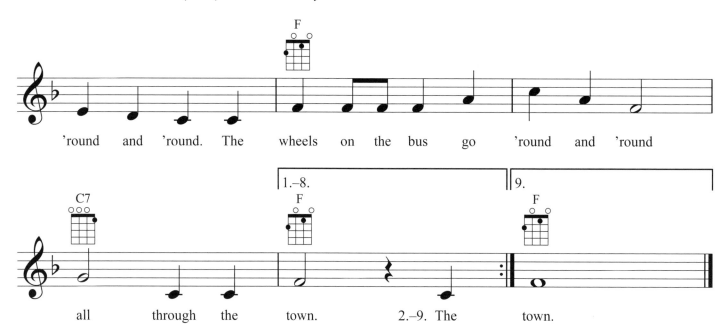

1. The wheels on the bus go 'round and 'round, 'round and 'round,
   (2.–9.) *See additional lyrics*

'round and 'round. The wheels on the bus go 'round and 'round

all through the town. 2.–9. The town.

Additional Lyrics

2. The wipers on the bus go swish, swish, swish,
   Swish, swish, swish, swish, swish swish.
   The wipers on the bus go swish, swish, swish
   All through the town.

3. The horn on the bus goes beep, beep, beep,
   Beep, beep, beep, beep, beep, beep.
   The horn on the bus goes beep, beep, beep
   All through the town.

4. The door on the bus goes open and shut,
   Open and shut, open and shut.
   The door on the bus goes open and shut
   All through the town.

5. The people on the bus go up and down,
   Up and down, up and down.
   The people on the bus go up and down
   All through the town.

6. The money on the bus goes clink, clink, clink,
   Clink, clink, clink, clink, clink, clink.
   The money on the bus goes clink, clink, clink
   All through the town.

7. The driver on the bus says, "Move on back,
   Move on back, move on back."
   The driver on the bus says, "Move on back,"
   All through the town.

8. The baby on the bus says, "Wah, wah, wah,
   Wah, wah, wah, wah, wah, wah."
   The baby on the bus says, "Wah, wah, wah,"
   All through the town.

9. The mommy on the bus says, "Shh, shh, shh,
   Shh, shh, shh, shh, shh, shh."
   The mommy on the bus says, "Shh, shh, shh,"
   All through the town.